FROM
SALVATION
to
SANCTIFICATION

D1692543

FROM
SALVATION

to

SANCTIFICATION

Then Eternal Life

*Although born in sin, humankind has been lovingly
granted the opportunity by God to be
saved, sanctified and filled with the Holy Spirit,
and ultimately spend eternal life
with Him.*

ZADIA B. TYSON

1603 Capitol Ave., Suite 310 Cheyenne, Wyoming USA 82001
1-888-980-6523 | admin@urlinkpublishing.com

URLink Print and Media is committed to excellence in the publishing industry.

Book design copyright © 2021 by URLink Print and Media. All rights reserved.

Published in the United States of America
Library of Congress Control Number: 2021904661
ISBN 978-1-64753-732-6 (Paperback)
ISBN 978-1-64753-733-3 (Digital)

23.02.20

THIS BOOK IS DEDICATED TO MY FAMILY

My husband, George Tyson, my children,
Beverly Shay and Michael Vanwen
My Grand Sweetheart, Breon C. Tyson

MY SISTERS
Mae Blanche, Lee Unice, Louise, Julia Mae and Daisy

MY BROTHER
Frank Oliver Garvin Lee Brown, Jr.
My Sister in Love, Josie Shellman Brown

TO THE LOVING MEMORIES OF
My beloved mother, Winnie A. Brown (my first teacher)
My brother, Tevis Brown,
And my Sister, Rosa Ellen B. Hall

TO THE UNFORGETTABLE MEMORIES
OF MY FIRST SUNDAY TEACHER
Mrs. "Miss Molly" Johnson

TO MY MOUNT CALVARY BAPTIST CHURCH FAMILY
Thank you for helping me grow and experience
God in His Holiness,

Especially to

My pastor/teacher, Reverend Anthony Burrell

The entire Christian Education Department, Members of Sunday
School Class #10; the Children's Church Workers; My dear friend,
Mrs. Lucille C. Scruggs; My Deacon and Deaconess Larry and Elsie
Seabrook; Deacon and Deaconess Malcolm and Deborah Roberts; and
to the very fond memories of my friend, Mrs. Catherine G. Johnson.

TO GOD BE THE GLORY FOR ALL THAT HE HAS DONE!!!

PREFACE

As a teacher of the median adult Sunday school class at Mount Calvary Baptist Church in Pompano Beach, Florida, I studied over the years to prepare to teach the class on Sunday mornings. I also attended weekly Bible Study, and as I studied, I learned to love and appreciate the revelation of what God is saying to us, His people; how He loves humankind so much that He saved us from our sins, and prepared for us to spend eternal life with Him.

As I began to work on this book, I realized Scriptures were imperative to support what I see as God bringing us from sinners to saints and, ultimately, spending eternal life with Him. Supportive Scriptures are used to verify each topic that is being discussed in the book. Some Scriptures are used more than once for verifications because many Scriptures do speak to more than one topic.

Unless indicated, all Scripture quotations come from the New International Version of the Holy Bible, as well as outline items. Quotations of definitions come from the Nelson's Illustrated Bible Dictionary.

As you begin your journey of reading this book, it is my sincere hope that you will receive the revelations that I have, and realize how richly blessed you are in Jesus Christ from birth to the grave and beyond. I trust that if you have not accepted Jesus Christ as your Lord and Savior, that you will do so, as a result of reading this book. If you are saved, but are not living a committed life to Christ, it is my prayer that you will make a commitment to do so by the time you have read this book in its entirety.

Being born into this world as a freewill agent, you have the awesome opportunity of making the choice where you will spend eternity. I trust in God you will make Him your choice!!
To God Be the Glory!

INTRODUCTION

"From Salvation to Sanctification; then Eternal Life" began in my backyard the spring of 2009. I was scheduled to host the "Friday Night Fish Fry" for my family reunion that was to be held the last weekend in July. In looking over my backyard, I decided to have some sprigs of grass put into a spot on the west side of my yard so that everything would look nice for the event. I took the responsibility of watering it myself and was quite proud when the grass seemed to be growing nice and thick. From a distance, it all looked the same. Being a novice to this kind of work, I thought everything was coming along nicely until one day, upon careful observation, I noticed that there were more weeds than grass in my yard. I was taking my dog, Gracie, out early every morning and as I was out anyway, I got the bright idea to start pulling up the weeds that were overpowering the grass. After pulling weeds for awhile and seeing some favorable results, I decided to sprig the whole backyard.

So that summer, I pulled weeds daily; but I noticed that as I pulled the weeds, the grass and the weeds continued to grow in together. One morning as I was pulling weeds, the Spirit of God spoke to my spirit that this is what sin is like in the life of a believer; it stunts their spiritual growth and they cannot become the people that He would have them be. Day after day, as I worked in my yard, those words resonated in my spirit. Then one morning, the Spirit of God spoke to my spirit that I should write about it.

It was at the end of the year that I decided to take on the task that was put upon me. Originally, in my mind, the book was to be titled, "Sin in the Life of the Christian," but as the work progressed, and by the leadership of the Holy Spirit, the title changed to, "From Salvation to Sanctification; then Eternal Life." This book begins with God, the Creator of all things. In His infinite wisdom, He created everything humankind could possibly need before He created man and woman. In His creation of humankind, He made no mistakes. He created man to be a freewill agent, one who could think for himself and then placed him in a perfect environment. Being a freewill agent, man had the choice to obey or disobey God. The choice to disobey God allowed sin to invade his perfect life.

Because of God's love for humankind, you will see the spiritual processes that God has afforded to us, His people, as we are transformed from sinners to saints, saved only by His grace. Man must deal with the sin in his life every day of his life. This is done only through making Jesus Christ the Lord and Savior of your life; ultimately being filled with the Holy Spirit, and intimately learning of God through His Word, the Holy Bible. After life in this world as we know it is over, as Christians, we will live with God in glorified bodies.

TABLE OF CONTENTS

CHAPTER ONE

CHAPTER TWO

CHAPTER THREE

CHAPTER FOUR

CHAPTER FIVE

CHAPTER SIX

CHAPTER SEVEN

Who Is God?

Who is God and where did He come from? Man has not been able to answer that age-old question, but for forever, men have believed and, therefore, know that God does exist and that He always will. He is not a physical being but is Spirit (John 4:24a). Being Spirit makes Him invisible. Therefore, there is no visible proof of His existence. There is no evidence of any kind that God has a beginning. He just is! He has no beginning and He is eternal. God told the prophet Isaiah to tell the people, "Before me no god was formed, nor will there be one after me," (Isaiah 43:10b). So man cannot physically see God; yet, he knows that this almighty, loving, kind, compassionate, forgiving, powerful and saving God does indeed exist.

The greatest revelation of God comes through studying the Bible. The Bible makes it perfectly clear that no man has ever seen God or can see Him. In writing to Timothy, the apostle Paul said:

> "God, the blessed and only Ruler, the King of kings and Lord of lords, who alone is immortal and who lives in unapproachable light, whom no one has seen or can see," (I Timothy 6:15-16).

God spoke through the prophets on many different occasions and in various ways to send His messages to the people of the Old Testament (Hebrews 1:1). Scriptures teach that the existence of God and His nature are revealed in and through His Son, Jesus Christ.

When Jesus taught His disciples that He was the way to the Father, He said:

> "I am the way and the truth and the life. No one comes to the Father except through Me. If you really knew Me, you would know my Father as well. From now on, you do know Him and have seen Him. Anyone who has seen me has seen the Father. The words I say to you are not just my own. Rather, it is the Father, living in me, who is doing His work. Believe me when I say that I am in the Father and the Father is in me; or at least believe on the evidence of the miracles themselves," (John 14:6-11).

Nature, in and all of its greatness reveals to humankind that there is a creator. Scriptures reveal that God is Creator of the universe by simply stating that, "In the beginning God created the heavens and the earth," (Genesis 1:1). God confirms this again when He inspired His prophet Isaiah to write, "I am the Lord, who has made all things, who alone stretched out the heavens, who spread out the earth by Myself," (Isaiah 44:24b). The apostle Paul wrote:

> "For since the creation of the world God's invisible qualities (His eternal power and divine nature) have been clearly seen, being understood from what has been made, so that men are without excuse," (Romans 1:20).

God also reveals Himself through the personal faith that man has acquired of Him through the study of the Bible that teaches of Him and His ways. In man's wildest imagination, he could not have dreamed of the insight and knowledge of God and His awesomeness all on his own. It had to come through the Spirit of God. God has always wanted humankind to know Him, believe in Him, and put His doctrines and principles into practice.

In order to know who God is and what He is to man, there must first be a desire to know Him and His way. God spoke to the prophet Jeremiah, saying: "I will give them a heart to know me, that I am the Lord," (Jeremiah 24:7). He inspired the apostle Paul to write in one of his letters, "I keep asking that the God of our Lord Jesus Christ, the glorious Father, may give to you the Spirit of wisdom and revelation, so that you may know Him better," (Ephesians 1:17). The Bible teaches that God is:

THE CREATOR

God's holy Word clearly states that He is the Creator of all things. He created the heavens and the earth out of nothing, as it was formless and empty (Genesis 1:2).The Bible does not tell us how He did it, but that He did it. According to the Scriptures, God spoke and everything came into existence (Genesis 1:3, 6, 11, 14, 20 and 24). The creation was done in an orderly fashion, and, according to the Bible, it took six days. We know that God was pleased with His creation because the Bible says, "God saw all that he had made, and it was very good," (Genesis 1:31a). In the Old and New Testaments, Scriptures speak of God as being Creator. God inspired Moses to write:

> "In the beginning God created the heavens and the earth. Now the earth was formless and empty, darkness was over the surface of the deep, and the Spirit of God was hovering over the water," (Genesis 1:1-2).

David, the psalmist, wrote:

> "I consider your heavens, the work of your fingers, the moon and stars which you have set in place," (Psalm 8:3).

An anonymous Psalmist wrote:

> "He set the earth on its foundations; it cannot be moved," (Psalm 104:5).

The prophet Isaiah wrote that God said:

> "It is I who made the earth and created man on it. My own hands stretched out the heaven; I marshaled their starry host," (Isaiah 45:12).

The apostle Paul wrote:

> "For by Him all things were created; things in heaven and on earth, visible and invisible, whether thrones or powers or rulers or authorities; all things were created by Him and for Him," (Colossians 1:16).

God, being the Creator of all things puts Him in authority of it all. His sovereignty makes Him in control of all nature, and He thereby provides for it. When things seem to get or even be out of control, man can be assured that the Lord God Almighty is in control of it all. This is true because the creation is never greater than the Creator. David, the psalmist, wrote:

> "You care for the land and water it; you enrich it abundantly. The streams of God are filled with water to provide the people with grain, for so you have ordained it. You drench its furrows and level its ridges; you soften it with showers and bless its crops. You crown the year with your bounty, and your carts overflow with abundance. The grasslands of the desert overflow; the hills are clothed with gladness. The meadows are covered with flocks and the valleys are mantled with grain. They shout for joy and sing," (Psalm 65:9-13).

The Bible gives a definite order for which God created the world. God instructed Moses to write of the account. He wrote that on the first day, God spoke day and night into existence when He said:

> "In the beginning God created the heaven and the earth. Now the earth was formless and empty, darkness was over the surface of the deep, and the Spirit of God was hovering over the waters. And God said, 'Let there be light,' and there was light. God saw that the light was good, and He separated the light from the darkness. He called the light 'day' and the darkness 'night.' And there was evening and morning the first day," (Genesis 1:1-5).

On the second day, God spoke the separation of the sea and sky. When He spoke the waters, which were under the firmament (the ocean, lakes, rivers, etc.), separated from the waters, which were above the firmament (waters in the clouds), He said:

> "Let there be an expanse between the waters to separate water from water." God called the expanse 'sky' and there was evening and morning," (Genesis 1:6-8).

On the third day, God spoke the separation of the land and water when He said:

> "Let the waters under the sky be gathered together unto one place, and let the dry ground appear. God called the dry ground 'land' and the gathered waters He called 'seas.' Then God said, 'Let the land produce vegetation: seed-bearing plants and trees on the land that bear fruit with seeds in it according to its own kinds,'" (Genesis 1:9-11).

On the fourth day, God spoke lights for the day and the night into existence when He said:

> "Let there be lights in the expanse of the sky to separate the day from the night, and let them serve as signs to mark seasons and days and years, and let them be lights in the expanse of the sky to give light on the earth. God made two great lights, the greater light to govern the day, and the lesser light to govern the night. He also made the stars. God set them in the expanse of the sky to give light on the earth, to govern the day and the night, and to separate light from darkness," (Genesis 1:14-18).

On the fifth day, God spoke creatures for the waters and birds for the air into existence when He said:

> "Let the water abound with an abundance of living creatures, and let birds fly above the earth across the face of the firmament of the heavens. So God created the great sea creatures and every living thing that moves, with which the waters abounded, according to their kind, and every winged bird according to its kind. Then God blessed them, saying, 'Be fruitful and multiply, and fill the water in the seas, and let birds multiply on the earth,'" (Genesis 1:20-22 NKJV).

On the sixth day, God spoke land creatures into existence when He said:

> "Let the land produce living creatures according to their kinds: livestock, creatures that move along the ground, and wild animals each according to its own kind," (Genesis 1:24).

It was also on this same day that God looked over His wonderful and beautiful creation, and saw that it was good. Man was not an afterthought, but that God planned everything in order. So when everything man needed to survive on earth was in its proper place, He created man. He said:

> "Let us make man in our image, in our likeness, and let them rule over the fish of the sea and the birds of the air, over the livestock, over all the earth, and over all the creatures that move along the ground," (Genesis 1:26).

And so, it was on this sixth day that God created both male and female in His own image and likeness. He then blessed them and said:

> "Be fruitful and increase in number; fill the earth and subdue it. Rule over the fish of the sea and the birds of the air and over every living creature that moves on the ground. I give you every seed-bearing plant on the face of the whole earth and every tree that has fruit with seed in it. They will be yours for food," (Genesis 1:28-30).

Now when God formed man from the dust of the earth, He did something unique to the man that He did not do with His other living creatures. He breathed into his nostrils the breath of life, and with that, man became a living being (Genesis 2:7). Man did not just become a physical being, but a spiritual one as well. As Solomon spoke about death, he said; "And the spirit returns to God who gave it," (Ecclesiastes 12:7b). Man is a body with a spirit and a soul. The apostle Paul said in his teachings:

> "May God Himself, the God of peace, sanctify you through and through. May your whole spirit, soul

and body be kept blameless at the coming of our Lord Jesus Christ," (I Thessalonians 5:23).

God placed Adam and Eve in the Garden of Eden with the responsibility to work it and take care of it. God told Adam that he was free to eat from any tree in the garden, as there were all kinds of trees there that were pleasing to the eye and good for food. The only tree he could not eat from was The Tree of the Knowledge of Good and Evil. Adam was told that if he did eat of that tree he would surely die (Genesis 2:8-9, 15-17).

God created a perfect world and apparently wanted everything to remain perfect. But He made Adam a free will agent, who had a mind to think for himself and make his own decisions. When God gave Adam the command not to eat from the tree, Adam was put in the position where he could obey God or disobey Him. Adam chose to disobey God when Eve, his wife, gave him fruit from The Tree of the Knowledge of Good and Evil to eat. Immediately after eating the fruit, they became aware of good and evil. Moses wrote:

> "When the woman saw that the fruit of the tree was good for food and pleasing to the eye, and also desirable for gaining wisdom, she took some and ate it. She also gave some to her husband, who was with her, and he ate. Then the eyes of both of them were opened, and they realized they were naked," (Genesis 3:6-7).

Life was perfect for them in the garden until they were tempted by the serpent, and sinned against God. Their disobedience brought a curse upon themselves as well as on the earth. When God approached them about their deeds, Adam blamed Eve, and Eve blamed the serpent by saying, "the serpent deceived me and I ate." Because God is a holy God and cannot tolerate sin, He had to punish Adam and Eve and the serpent as well. He said to the serpent:

"Cursed are you above all the livestock and all the wild animals! You will crawl on your belly and you will eat dust all the days of your life. And I will put enmity between you and the woman, and between you and your offspring and hers; He will crush your head, and you will strike His heel," (Genesis 3:14, 15).

For Eve's punishment, God said to her:

"I will greatly increase your pain in childbearing; with pain you will give birth to children. Your desire will be for your husband, and he will rule over you," (Genesis 3:16).

For Adam's punishment, God said to him:

"Because you listened to your wife and ate from the tree about which I commanded you, 'You must not eat of it.' Cursed is the ground because of you; through painful toil you will eat of it all the days of your life. It will produce thorns and thistles for you and you will eat plants of the field. By the sweat of your brow you will eat your food until you return to the ground, since from it you were taken; for dust you are and to dust you will return," (Genesis 3:17-19).

Man was very special to God because he was created in God's own image and likeness. This "image" put man into a different category, separate from the other living creatures. He possesses qualities that are unique only to man. He is able to think and communicate; he is able to discern right from wrong; he has a conscience; he has emotions and he has the capability to worship God. Because God created man to live upright and do what is right (Ecclesiastes 7:29), He provided him with everything he needed to live a good life. David, the psalmist, wrote that God the Creator esteemed His most valuable creation-man when he wrote:

> "What is man that you are mindful of him, the son of man that you care for him? You made him a little lower than the heavenly beings and crowned him with glory and honor. You made him ruler over the works of your hands; You put everything under his feet; all flocks and herds, and the beasts of the field, the birds of the air, and the fish of the sea, all that swim the paths of the seas," (Psalm 8:4-8).

Another age-old question is still being asked today; "Why did God create humankind and what is their purpose on earth?" In certain of the Old and New Testament Scriptures, God tells why He created humankind beginning in the Book of Genesis.

HIS REASONS FOR CREATING HUMANKIND

To Rule Over the Earth

Moses wrote that after God had created everything, He said:

> "Let us create man in our image, in our likeness, and let them rule over the fish of the sea and birds of the air, over the livestock, over all the earth and over all the creatures that move along the ground." God blessed them and said to both the male and female; "Be fruitful and increase in number; fill the earth and subdue it," (Genesis 1:26-30).

To Obey God

God put Adam in the Garden of Eden to work it and take care of it. Then the Lord commanded the man:

"You are free to eat from any tree in the garden; but you must not eat from the Tree of Knowledge of Good and Evil, for when you eat of it you will surely die," (Genesis 2:15-17).

The prophet Micah told the people:

"He has showed you, O man, what is good. And what does the Lord require of you? Act justly and to love mercy and to walk humbly with your God," (Micah 6:8).

In the New Testament, Jesus said:

"It is written: 'Man does not live on bread alone, but by every word that comes from the mouth of God," (Matthew 4:4).

In his writings, the apostle Paul gave several reasons as to why God created man. He wrote:

To Be Adopted as His Sons

"He predestined us to be adopted as His sons through Jesus Christ, in accordance with His pleasure and will, to the praise of His glorious grace, which He has freely given us in the One He loves," (Ephesians 1:5-6).

To Become in the Likeness of Jesus Christ

"For those God foreknew he also predestined to be conformed to the likeness of His Son," (Romans 8:29a).

To Please God

"So we make it our goal to please Him, whether we are at home in the body or away from it," (2 Corinthians 5:9a).

To Do Good Work

"For we are God's workmanship, created in Christ Jesus to do good work, which God prepared in advance for us to do," (Ephesians 2:10).

To Become Saved and Come into the Knowledge of His Truth

"God wants all men to be saved and come to the knowledge of the truth. There is one God and one mediator between God and men, the Christ Jesus, who gave Himself as a ransom for all men," (1Timothy 2:4-6b).

To Be Holy

"He chose us in Him before the creation of the world to be holy and blameless in His sight," (Ephesians 1:4).

"But just as He who called is holy, so be holy in all that you do, for it is written: 'Be holy, because I am holy,'" (I Peter 1:15-16).

Adam and Eve's disobedience brought sin into the world. Every human being ever born, with the exception of Jesus, has inherited the sinful nature of them. Adam's sin set in place the reign of death. The apostle Paul wrote:

"Therefore, just as sin entered the world through one man, and death through sin, and in this way death came to all men, because all sinned." He further stated, "Consequently, just as the result of Adam's sin was condemnation for all men," (Romans 5:12, 18).

God wanted a perfect world, where man would love and obey Him. However, sin caused the whole picture to change. Disobedience to God by Adam and Eve is the reason people are sinful and not what God created them to be. As a result of their sins, humankind is basically evil. God said that the inclination of man's heart is evil from his childhood (Genesis 8:21). Old and New Testament writers wrote of man being sinful and evil. David, the psalmist said:

"There is no fear of God before his eyes. For in his own eye he flatters himself too much to detect or hate his sin. The words of his mouth are wicked and deceitful; he has ceased to be wise and to do good. Even on his bed he plots evil. He commits himself to a sinful course and does not reject what is wrong," (Psalm 36:1-4).

"Surely I was sinful at birth, sinful from the time my mother conceived me," (Psalm 51:5).

"Even from birth the wicked go astray, from the womb they are wayward and speak lies," (Psalm 58:3).

The Lord said to the prophet Jeremiah:

"The heart is deceitful above all things and beyond cure. Who can understand it?" (Jeremiah 17:9).

In the New Testament, Scriptures tell that man, God's greatest creation has not been able to live up to God's expectations. Matthew recorded that Jesus said:

"For out of the heart come evil thoughts, murder, adultery, sexual immorality, theft, false testimony, slander. These are what make a man 'unclean,'" (Matthew 15:19).

The apostle Paul wrote:

"The sinful mind is hostile to God. It does not submit to God's law, nor can it do so. Those controlled by the sinful nature cannot please God," (Romans 8:7-8).

God is known as the Great Creator of the heavens and earth. He is also known to have many other characteristics or attributes.

GOD IS SPIRIT

"God cannot be described in a comprehensive way, but man can learn about Him by examining His attributes as revealed in the Bible," (Nelson's Illustrated Bible Dictionary, 1986). The first group of attributes talk about what is is natural about Him. Jesus taught that God is Spirit when he wrote: "God is Spirit, and His worshipers must worship in spirit and truth," (John 4:24).

He is not a physical being with limitations. He cannot be seen with the naked eye, which makes Him invisible. He has no body, nor form. And according to the Word of God, He has no beginning and no end. Old and New Testament Scriptures support the fact that God is Spirit. Moses wrote from the beginning of time that God is Spirit when he said:

"The earth was formless and empty, darkness was over the surface of the deep, and the Spirit of God was hovering over the waters," (Genesis 1:2).

David, the psalmist, said to the Lord:

> "Where can I go from your Spirit? Where can I flee
> from your presence?" (Psalm 139:7).

John the Baptist gave this testimony at Jesus' baptism:

> "I saw the Spirit come down from heaven as a dove
> and remain on Him," (John 1:32b).

GOD IS IMMUTABLE

"Immutability is a characteristic of God's nature which means that He does not change in His basic nature," (Nelson's Illustrated Bible Dictionary). He is the same at all times. He does not deviate from being one kind of God to another. If He did, He would not be the perfect God that He is. New Testament writers wrote of God's immutability. The unknown author of the Book of Hebrews said:

> "In the beginning, O Lord, You laid the foundations
> of the earth, and the heavens are the work of your
> hands. They will perish, but you remain; they will
> all wear out like a garment. You will roll them up
> like a robe; like a garment they will be changed. But
> you remain the same, and your years will never end,"
> (Hebrews 1:10-12).

James, the brother of Jesus wrote:

> "Every good and perfect gift is from above, coming
> down from the Father of the heavenly lights, who does
> not change like sifting shadows," (James 1:17).

GOD IS OMNIPOTENT

"Omnipotence is a theological term that refers to the all-encompassing power of God." His power is unlimited, which makes Him a sovereign God. He can do all things and everything. He is in control of everything that is and was and is to come. "God reveals in the Bible that He is all-powerful and in the final sense is the ruler of nature and history," (Nelson's Illustrated Bible Dictionary). Scriptures in both the Old and New Testaments tell of His omnipotence. Moses wrote:

> "God caused it to rain for forty days and forty nights to destroy all living things on earth," (Genesis 7:4).

> God allowed 100-year-old Abraham and his 90-year-old wife to bear a child (Genesis 21:1-5).

> God parted the Red Sea so that the Israelites were able to walk on dry land to escape the Egyptian soldiers and Egyptian bondage (Exodus 14:14-16).

In the midst of all his troubles, Job said to the Lord:

> "I know that you can do all things; no plan of yours can be thwarted," (Job 42:1).

King Solomon wrote in his proverbs of wisdom:

> "In his heart a man plans his course, but the Lord determines his steps," (Proverbs 16:9).

> "There is no wisdom, no insight, no plan that can succeed against the Lord," (Proverbs 21:30).

The prophet Isaiah wrote that God said:

> "No one can deliver out of my hand. When I act, who can reverse it," (Isaiah 43:13b)?

This is what the prophet Daniel said about God's power:

> "He changes times and seasons; He sets up kings and deposes them. He gives wisdom to the wise and knowledge to the discerning," (Daniel 2:21).

After a conversation with the rich man about eternal life, Jesus said to his disciples:

> "With man this is impossible, but with God all things are possible," (Matthew 19:26).

Luke, the Gospel writer records that God sent the angel Gabriel to the Virgin Mary, who was engaged to marry a man named Joseph. The angel approached Mary and said:

> "You will be with child and give birth to a Son, and you are to give Him the name Jesus. The Holy Spirit will come upon you, and the power of the Most High will overshadow you. So, the Holy one to be born will be called the Son of God. Even Elizabeth your relative is going to have a child in her old age, and she who was said to be barren is in her sixth month. Nothing is impossible with God," (Luke 1:31, 35-37).

GOD IS OMNIPRESENT

"Omnipresence is a theological term that is refers to the unlimited nature of God or His ability to be everywhere at all times. He reveals Himself in the Bible as the Lord who is everywhere. He is the Creator and Sustainer of time and space, He is everywhere," (Nelson's

Illustrated Bible Dictionary). As Creator, He has a bird's eye view of everything that happens on earth. Therefore, there are no hiding places on this earth from God as He is everywhere. The omnipresence of God was written about in both the Old and New Testaments. The psalmist, David, wrote:

> "Where can I go from your Spirit? Where can I flee from your presence? If I go up to the heavens, you are there; if I make my bed in the depths, you are there. If I rise on the wings of the dawn, if I settle on the far side of the sea, even there your hand will guide me, your right hand will hold me fast," (Psalm 139:7-12).

King Solomon wrote in one of his proverbs:

> "The eyes of the Lord are everywhere, keeping watch on the wicked and the good," (Proverbs 15:3).

The prophet Jeremiah recorded that God asked the questions:

> "Am I only a God nearby, and not a God far away? Can anyone hide in secret places so that I cannot see him? Do not I fill heaven and earth?" (Jeremiah 23:23-24).

Jesus said this of God's omnipresence:

> "When you pray, go into your room, close the door and pray to your Father, who is unseen. Then your Father, who sees what is done is secret, will reward you," (Matthew 6:6).

GOD IS OMNISCIENT

"Omniscience is a theological term that refers to God's superior knowledge and wisdom, His power to know all things," (Nelson's Illustrated Bible Dictionary). He has knowledge of the past, present and future because He created time. With His all knowing power, He knows everything about people. He knows their thoughts before they are ever spoken, and knows what they are going to do before it is ever done. Scriptures writers in both the Old and New Testaments wrote of God's omniscience. During Job's discourse, he asked a question, then, answered the question when he said:

> "Where does wisdom come from, and where does understanding dwell?" He answered it by saying; "It is hidden from the eyes of every living thing, concealed even from the birds of the air. God understands the way to it and He alone knows where it dwells, for He views the ends of the earth and sees everything under the heavens," (Job 28:20-21, 23-24).

An anonymous psalmist said:

> "From the heaven the Lord looks down and sees all mankind; from His dwelling place He watches all who live on earth-He who forms the hearts of all, who considers everything they do," (Psalm 33:13-15).

In one of David's psalms, he said:

> "O Lord, you searched me and you know me. You know when I sit and when I rise; you perceive my thoughts from afar. You discern my going out and my lying down; you are familiar with all my ways. Before a word is on my tongue you know it completely," (Psalm 139:1-4, 13).

In praise to God, the prophet Daniel said:

> "He reveals deep and hidden things; He knows what lies in darkness," (Daniel 2:22).

God spoke of His omniscience when He told the prophet Jeremiah:

> "My eyes are on all their ways; they are not hidden from me, nor is their sin concealed from my eyes," (Jeremiah 16:17).

During Jesus' teachings, He said:

> "And even the very hairs of your head are numbered," (Matthew 10:30).

The author of Hebrews wrote:

> "Nothing in all creation is hidden from God's sight. Everything is uncovered and laid bare before the eyes of Him to whom we must give account," (Hebrews 4:13).

GOD IS ETERNAL

God is eternal in nature. He is the beginning and there is no end to Him. In Hebrews 1:11-12, the author writes that when earth and heaven perishes, which is the work of God's hands, He will remain the same, and His years will never end. He is the eternal ruler over the past, present and future, and therefore, has no limitations. He said, "I am the Alpha and the Omega, who is, and who was, and who is to come, the Almighty," (Revelation 1:8). In a prayer to God in the oldest Psalm, realizing His eternality, Moses said:

> "Lord, you have been our dwelling place throughout all generations. Before the mountains were born or

you brought forth the earth and the world, from everlasting to everlasting, you are God. A thousand years in your sight are like a day that has just gone by, or like a watch in the night," (Psalm 90:1-2, 4).

"The second group of attributes of God is called moral attributes. These refer to God's character, His essential nature," (Nelson's Illustrated Bible Dictionary, 1986).

GOD IS LOVE

The apostle John said, "God is love," and He is the source of love. God showed Himself to be love when He sent His beloved Son, Jesus Christ, down to earth to die for the sins of the world that they may have eternal life (I John 4:8b-9). God's love expresses the essential self-giving nature of Himself. Man was created so that God would have someone to express His love too. Love originated from God and is unconditional. He loves humankind in spite of their imperfections. This will never change because He is the God of love. In both the Old and New Testaments, authors wrote of God's love for humankind. An anonymous psalmist wrote:

> "For the Lord is good and His love endures forever;
> His faithfulness continues through all generations,"
> (Psalm 100:5).

The prophet Jeremiah wrote in the midst of afflictions:

> "Because of the Lord's great love we are not consumed,
> for His compassions never fail," (Lamentations 3:22).

The apostle John wrote that Jesus said:

> "For God so loved the world that He gave His one
> and only Son, that whoever believes in Him shall not
> perish but have eternal life," (John 3:16).

He also said in his first letter:

> "Dear friends, let us love one another, for love comes from God. Everyone who loves has been born of God and knows God. Whoever does not love does not know God, because God is love," (I John 4:7-8)

GOD IS HOLY

"Holiness describes God's righteous nature. Originating in God's nature, holiness is a unique quality of His character. It refers to His moral excellence. He sets the standards for morality, because of His holiness," (Nelson Illustrated Bible Dictionary). It is because of His holiness that He cannot contend with sin in His people, although He loves them unconditionally. Scripture writers in both the Old and New Testaments wrote of God's holiness. God instructed Moses to tell the people that He said:

> "I am the Lord your God; consecrate yourselves and be holy, because I am holy. I am the Lord who brought you up out of Egypt to be your God; therefore be holy, because I am holy," (Leviticus 11:44a and 45).

An anonymous psalmist wrote:

> "Exalt the Lord our God and worship at His footstool; He is holy." In the same chapter of praise, he said; "Exalt the Lord our God and worship at His holy mountain, for the Lord our God is holy," (Psalm 99:5, 9).

The apostle Peter wrote in his first letter to God's people everywhere:

> "As obedient children, do not conform to the evil desires you had when you lived in ignorance. But just as He who called you is holy, so be holy in all you do;

for it is written: 'Be holy because I am holy,'" (I Peter 1:14-16).

GOD IS FAITHFUL

Faithfulness is another one of God's key attributes. God will honor His promises and fulfill His Word. There is no failure in God and His Word. He will do whatever He says He will do. In teaching on God's faithfulness, Paul asked the question, "What if some did not have faith? Will their lack of faith nullify God's faithfulness?" He answered his question by saying, "Not at all! Let God be true, and every man be a liar," (Romans 3:3-4a). God's faithfulness is spoken of in both the Old and New Testaments. While speaking to Moses in this passage, God said of Himself:

> "The Lord, the Lord, the compassionate and gracious God, is slow to anger, abounding in love and faithfulness," (Exodus 34:6).

David, the psalmist, said:

> "The Lord is faithful to all His promises and loving toward all that He has made" (Psalm 145:13b).

The apostle Paul said:

> "No temptation has seized you except what is common to man. And God is faithful; He will not let you be tempted beyond what you can bear. But when you are tempted, He will also provide a way out so that you can stand up under it," (1 Corinthians 10:13).

> "If we are faithless, He will remain faithful, for He cannot disown Himself," (2Timothy 2:13).

GOD IS FORGIVING

Forgiveness has always been a part of God's nature. Forgiveness is the act of excusing someone for their shortcomings. God's love for humankind causes Him to forgive sinners and accept them as His own. No sin is so bad that it cannot be forgiven. When He forgives man of his sins, He does not count the sins against him anymore. David said, "Blessed is the man whose sin the Lord does not count against him and in whose spirit is no deceit," (Psalm 32:2). God wants to forgive people for their sins, but they must first truly repent of their wrong doings. Scripture writers wrote of God's desire to forgive man for his sins. The Lord appeared to King Solomon one night and said:

> "If my people, who are called by my name, will humble themselves and pray and seek my face and turn from their wicked ways, then will I hear from heaven and will forgive their sin and will heal their land," (2 Chronicles 7:14).

David said:

> "Praise the Lord, O my soul, and forget not all His benefits. He forgives all your sins and heals all your diseases," (Psalm 103:2-3).

An anonymous psalmist wrote:

> "If you, O Lord, kept a record of sins, O Lord who could stand? But with you there is forgiveness," (Psalm 130:3-4a).

Jesus taught on forgiveness. While teaching His disciple how to pray, He said:

"For if you forgive men when they sin against you, your heavenly Father will also forgive you," (Matthew 6:14).

The author of Hebrews wrote that God said:

"Their sins and lawless acts, I will remember no more," (Hebrews 10:17).

The apostle John wrote:

"If we confess our sins, He is faithful and just and will forgive us our sins, and purify us from all unrighteousness," (I John 1:9).

GOD IS GOOD

It is of God's character to be good. God's goodness consists of righteousness, holiness, justice, kindness, grace, mercy and love. The expression "God is good all the time, and all the time God is good" is used loosely by many, but it is a profound and true statement that should be spoken with love and authority by the believer. God shows Himself to be good to all His creations. Old and New Testament writers recorded passages pertaining to the goodness of God. God spoke of His goodness when He said to Moses:

"I will cause all my goodness to pass in front of you, and I will proclaim my name, the Lord, in your presence," (Exodus 33:19).

"The Lord, the Lord God, merciful and gracious, longsuffering and abounding in goodness and truth," (Exodus 34:6NKJV).

Jesus said to Peter;

> "No one is good-except God alone," (Mark 10:18).

The apostle Peter said:

> "Like newborn babies, crave pure spiritual milk, so
> that by it you may grow up in your salvation, now that
> you have tasted that the Lord is good," (1 Peter 2:2-3).

GOD IS GRACE

"Grace is one of the key attributes of God. It is the favor or
kindness, shown without regard to the worth or merit of the one
who receives it and in spite of what the same person deserves,"
(Nelson's Illustrated Bible Dictionary). The grace of God is applied
to humankind for their salvation by their faith in the birth, death, and
resurrection of Jesus Christ. God's grace is a free gift to humankind.
It cannot be earned, but is voluntarily given to those He saves. God's
grace is for everyone, and without it, nobody can be saved. Scriptures
teach that grace is almost always associated with mercy, love and
compassion, when there is a need for help or deliverance. Old and
New Testament Scriptures reveal the graciousness of God. The Lord
God said to Moses:

> "The Lord, the Lord, the compassionate and
> gracious God is slow to anger, abounding in love and
> faithfulness," (Exodus 34:6).

An anonymous psalmist wrote:

> "The Lord is gracious and righteous; our God is full
> of compassion," (Psalm 116:5).

The apostle Paul wrote:

> "To the praise of His glorious grace, which He has freely given us in the One He loves. In Him we have redemption through His blood, the forgiveness of sins, in accordance with the riches of God's grace that He lavished on us with all wisdom and understanding," (Ephesians 1:6-8).

GOD IS MERCIFUL

"Mercy is the aspect of God's love that causes Him to help those that are guilty of breaking His law and do not deserve His help, but instead deserves punishment," (Nelson's Illustrated Bible Dictionary). David, the psalmist said:

> "He does not treat us as our sins deserve or repay us, according to our iniquities. For as high as the heavens are above the earth, so great is His love for those who fear Him; as far as the east is from the west, so far has He removed our transgressions from us" (Psalm 103:10-12).

When man sins against God, he cannot demand God's mercy or initiate it. It is out of love that God shows mercy for him. The Lord said to Moses, "I will have mercy on whom I will have mercy, and I will have compassion on whom I will have compassion," (Exodus 33:19b). Certain other Old and New Testament writers wrote of God and His mercy, based on what they knew of Him. The psalmist David reminded God of His mercifulness when he said:

> "Remember, O lord, your great mercy and love, for they are from old," (Psalm 25:6).

An anonymous psalmist wrote:

> "I love the Lord, for He heard my voice; he heard my cry for mercy. Because He turned His ear to me, I will call on Him as long as I live," (Psalm 116:1-2).

In one of the Prophet Daniel's prayers, he said:

> "We do not make requests of you because we are righteous, but because of your great mercy," (Daniel 9:18b).

After the Virgin Mary accepted the fact that she was chosen to be the mother of Jesus, the Savior of the world, she referred to God and His mercifulness as she used these words in her song:

> "His mercy extends to those who fear him, from generation to generation," (Luke 1:50).

Jesus taught His disciples:

> "Be merciful, just as your Father is merciful," (Luke 6:36).

GOD IS RIGHTEOUS

"The righteousness of God refers to His moral laws laid down to guide the conduct of humankind, as in the Ten Commandments," (Nelson's Illustrated Bible Dictionary). God's righteousness is always the same. He affirms what is right and rejects what is wrong. In His righteousness, He cannot and will not tolerate sin. The Bible tells of writers in both the Old and New Testaments who wrote or sang of God's righteousness, as well as others of God's prophets who wrote what God told them to say about His righteousness. David recorded:

"The Lord is righteous in all His ways and loving toward all He has made," (Psalm 145:17).

An anonymous writer of the psalms wrote:

"Glorious and majestic are his deeds, and His righteousness endures forever," (Psalm 111:3).

The prophet Isaiah said the Lord said:

"And there is no God apart from me, a righteous God and a savior," (Isaiah 45:21b).

The apostle John wrote to the children of God:

"Dear Children, do not let anyone lead you astray. He who does what is right is righteous, just as He is righteous," (1 John 3:7).

GOD IS TRUTH

"Truth is a fundamental moral and personal quality of God," (Nelson's Illustrated Bible Dictionary). In His perfect nature, God acts in truth, and speaks the truth. He is true to man and true to His Word. He is a God that cannot lie. Moses said, "God is not a man, that He should lie, nor a Son of Man, that He should change His mind. Does He speak and then not act? Does He promise and not fulfill?" (Numbers 23:19). Scriptures in the Old and New Testaments tell of writers who wrote of God's truthfulness as they had experienced it. In the song of Moses, he said:

"He is the Rock, His work is perfect; for all His ways are justice, a God of truth and without injustice; righteous and upright is He," (Deuteronomy 32:4 NKJV).

David, the psalmist, wrote:

> "Into Your hands I commit my spirit; redeem me, O Lord, the God of truth," (Psalm 31:5).

Jesus said to His disciples:

> "I am the way, and the truth and the life. No one comes to the Father except through Me," (John 14:6).

The author of the Book of Hebrews wrote:

> "Because God wanted to make the unchanging nature of His purpose very clear to the heirs of what was promised, he confirmed it with an oath. God did this so that by two unchangeable things in which it is impossible for God to lie," (Hebrews 6:17-18a).

GOD IS PEACE

"Peace often refers to the inner tranquility and poise of the Christian whose trust is in God through Christ. It is the quietness in the mind and soul, brought about by the reconciliation with God," (Nelson Illustrated Bible Dictionary). God desires peace for His people, and gives it. In the midst of mass confusion, God's people can have a complete peace of mind, given only by Him. This peace that God gives is more than a feeling of calmness and tranquility. It comes at another level in man's relationship with God. The apostle Paul assured his listeners of God's peace when he said:

> "Whatever you have learned or received or heard from me, or seen in me, put it into practice. And the God of peace will be with you," (Philippians 4:9).

OTHER NAMES FOR GOD

"God favored His people by revealing Himself to His people by several names which offered insight into His love and righteousness. One of the most important names for God in the Old Testament is Yahweh, or Jehovah from the verb 'to be,' meaning simply but profoundly, 'I am who I am,' and 'I will be who I will be,'" (Nelson's Illustrated "Bible Dictionary). In the Old Testament, He is also frequently referred to as "Lord," "Almighty" and "Most High."

Lord

The word "Lord" is translated from the word "Yahweh." The Jewish people considered the name "Yahweh" too holy for human lips, so instead they used the word Lord as another name for God. Today, the words "God" and "Lord" are used interchangeably. Both names tell of His loving nature. In the Old Testament, God referred to Himself as Lord as He spoke to His prophets with messages for His people. In talking to Moses about His name He said:

> "I AM WHO I AM. This is what you are to say to the Israelites: 'I AM has sent me to you. The Lord, the God of your fathers, the God of Abraham, the God of Isaac and the God of Jacob has sent me to you. This is my name by which I am to be remembered from generation to generation,'" (Exodus 3:13-15).

As God was giving Moses the Ten Commandments, He said:

> "You shall not misuse the name of the Lord your God, for the Lord will not hold anyone guiltless who misuses His name," (Exodus20:7).

He also said:

> "I, the Lord your God, am a jealous God,"
> (Deuteronomy 5:9).

The prophet Isaiah wrote:

> "Yet the Lord longs to be gracious to you; He rises
> to show you compassion. For the Lord is a God of
> justice. Blessed are all who wait for Him," (Isaiah
> 30:18).

Almighty

The name "Almighty" is used to show God as a source of blessings and being able to meet the needs of all people. Nothing is impossible with Him! Old Testament writers wrote of God Almighty. One psalmist said:

> "O Lord God Almighty, who is like you? You are
> mighty, O Lord, and your faithfulness surrounds
> you," (Psalm 89:8).

In a prayer that Jeremiah prayed, he said:

> "O great and powerful God, whose name is the Lord
> Almighty, great are your purposes and mighty are
> your deeds," (Jeremiah 32:18b-19a).

Most High

The Most High is a name for God, which appears frequently in the Old Testament. This name emphasizes God's might and power. He is sovereign. He is above everything and everyone, and has no limitations. An anonymous psalmist said:

"He who dwell in the shelter of the Most High will rest in the shadow of the Almighty," (Psalm 91:1).

The prophet Daniel saw in a vision a messenger, a holy one, coming down out of heaven. He said, in part, to him:

"The decision is announced by messengers, the holy ones declare the verdict, so that the living may know that the Most High is sovereign over the kingdoms of men and gives them to anyone He wishes and sets over them the lowliest of men,"(Daniel 4:17).

Father

Once man accepts Jesus Christ as his Savior, God becomes his heavenly Father. He is personal to each and every believer in Christ because they are now a part of His family in which He is the Father. In the Old and New Testaments, God is referred to as Father. In one of David's psalms, he said God is:

"A father to the fatherless, a defender of widows, is God in His holy habitation," (Psalm 68:5).

During praise, the prophet Isaiah said to God:

"But you are our Father, though Abraham does not know us or Israel acknowledge us; you, O Lord, are our Father," (Isaiah 63:16).

Jesus acknowledged God as His Father when He prayed. He said:

"I praise you, Father, Lord of heaven and earth, because you have hidden these things from the wise and learned, and revealed them to little children. Yes, Father, for this was your good pleasure," (Matthew 11:25-26).

When Jesus warned His disciples against the religious leaders, He said:

> "Do not call anyone on earth 'father,' for you have one Father, and He is in heaven," (Matthew 23:9).

Abba Father

"Abba is an Aramaic word which corresponds to our 'Daddy' or 'Papa," (Nelson's Illustrated Bible Dictionary). Upon accepting Jesus Christ as Lord and Savior, man is adopted into the family of God. As His adopted child, he becomes an heir to what God has and can claim what God has for him. As the apostle Paul taught on being the sons of God, he said:

> "Those who are led by the Spirit of God are sons of God. For you did not receive a spirit that makes you a slave again to fear, but you received the Spirit of sonship. And by Him we cry, 'Abba, Father,'" (Romans 8:14-15).

God, in His awesomeness and infinite wisdom, first created the world; then man, whom He gave a special place in it. After the six days of creation, God was pleased because everything He created was good and very good. God had high expectations of man because He created him in His own image, and made him ruler over all the other creations. After Adam and Eve's disobedience to God, the following generations of theirs became more and more rebellious against God until evilness was over the whole world. Moses said that God saw how great man's wickedness on the earth had become, and that every inclination of the thoughts of his heart were evil all the time. God's heart was filled with pain, and He was grieved that He had made man on the earth. Moses recorded that God said:

"I will wipe mankind, whom I have created from the face of the earth-men and animals, and creatures that move along the ground, and birds of the air-for I am grieved that I made them," (Genesis 6:5-7).

The whole earth was filled with people involved in all kinds of sinful acts and wickedness. God being a holy, righteous, and a just God, could not overlook their sins, but He still wanted humankind to inhabit the earth. He knew of only one man that He could save and use him to become the second father of the human race, and that was Noah. He saw Noah as a righteous man, blameless among the people of his time, and he walked with God (Genesis 6:8-9). This does not mean that Noah never sinned, but just that he loved and obeyed God.

According to Scriptures, Noah became the vessel God used to save mankind from total destruction. God told Noah that He was going to destroy all the people, because the earth is filled with violence because of them. He instructed Noah to build a boat. He gave him the dimensions for the boat along with the instructions on how to build it. Then God told him that he was going to bring floodwaters on earth to destroy all life on earth. He said everything on earth will die. God then told him to enter into the Ark with his wife, his three sons and their wives. God told him that he should bring into the ark two of all living creatures, male and female, clean and unclean, and keep them alive with him. That included birds and every kind of creature that moves along on the ground. Noah was also instructed to bring in every kind of food to be eaten by him and the animals. Noah did everything just as God commanded him to do in order to repopulate the earth (Genesis 6:13-22).

Noah obviously appeared foolish to all the people around him because there was no water around them for a boat. God then told him that in seven days He would send rain on the earth for forty days and forty nights, and that He would wipe every living creature that He had made from the face of the earth. Noah did all that God commanded him and God shut them in the Ark. After seven days as

God had said, the rain came down on earth for forty days and forty nights (Genesis 7:4-12, 16).

After the flood, God blessed Noah and his sons. He said to them, "Be fruitful and increase in number and fill the earth." God made a covenant with Noah and his sons. He said, "Never again will all life be cut off by the waters of a flood; never again will there be a flood to destroy the earth," (Genesis 9:1, 11). Although all the evil people had been destroyed, the sinful nature of man was still present. Noah, a godly man, got drunk from wine, and one of his sons looked upon his nakedness (Genesis 9:21). God had judged sin on the earth, and started another generation of people; yet, the sinful nature of the people was very much alive.

CHAPTER TWO

Sin

"Sin is lawlessness, or transgression of God's will, either by omitting to do what God's Law requires or by doing what it forbids," (Nelson's Illustrated Bible Dictionary). Since the fall of Adam and Eve in the Garden, all of humankind is born in sin and therefore has a sinful nature. The apostle John wrote, "If we claim to be without sin, we deceive ourselves and the truth is not in us," (1 John 1:8). The truth of the matter is, all men have sinned and fall short of the glory of God (Romans 3:23).

James, the brother of Jesus said, "Anyone who knows the good he ought to do and doesn't do it, sins," (James 4:17). So what makes sin so powerful that it is able to separate man from God, his Creator? After all, God saw man as His most valuable creation because He created him in His own image and likeness. Adam and Eve lived in a perfect world and had a perfect relationship with God, but they made the choice to disobey God's command. God put Adam in the Garden of Eden to work it and take care of it. He specifically said to Adam:

> "You are free to eat from any tree in the garden; but you must not eat from The Tree of the Knowledge of Good and Evil, for when you eat from it you will surely die," (Genesis 2:15-17).

It was God's desire that Adam obeyed Him, but Adam chose to do the opposite of what God told him to do. Since the fall of Adam and Eve in the Garden, man has been disobedient to the Word of

God. He seems to underestimate the result of sin in his life. He refers to some sins as "little," while other sins are referred to as "big." God sees all sin as sin, even unintentional sins. All sin separates man from the love of God, even those that are referred to as "little sins." Since all wrongdoings in the sight of God are sins, He cannot and will not ignore them because of His holiness.

VARIOUS TYPES OF SINS

Error – To error is make a mistake.

Lawlessness - Lawlessness is rebellious behavior.

Iniquity - Iniquity is to do those things that are unrighteous or unlawful.

Transgression - Transgression is to violate a law or command; to do what is not right, and being aware of it.

Trespass - Trespass is moving away from the right path; failing to meet God's standards.

THE EFFECTS OF SIN IN HUMANKIND

The disobedience of Adam in the Garden of Eden brought sin into the world. The apostle Paul wrote: "Therefore, just as sin entered the world through one man, and death through sin, and in this way death came to all men, because all sinned,"(Romans 5:12). Satan, the deceiver was present in the Garden of Eden, and it was he who used temptations to get Eve to sin. He was disguised as a serpent and purposefully came to tempt her by telling her what she wanted to hear. After being enticed by Satan, she then got Adam involved. Satan was successful in causing God's first two people to sin and has been tempting people to sin every since.

Sin begins in the heart of man. The prophet Jeremiah said: "The heart is deceitful above all things and beyond cure. Who can understand it?" (Jeremiah 17:9). Why is Satan so successful in getting people to sin against God their Creator? In the Old and New Testaments, God gives Scriptures that teach what sin is as well as the results of it in the lives of people. The Bible teaches that sin:

Encourages People to Ignore God's Commands

God told Adam not to eat from the one special tree in the Garden of Eden. The serpent enticed Eve to eat of it, and she gave some to Adam, her husband, who was with her (Genesis 2:16-17; 3:1-6). She ignored what God had said when Satan told her:

> "You will not surely die, for God knows that when you eat of it your eyes will be opened, and you will be like God, knowing good and evil," (Genesis 3:4).

Breaks Fellowship with God

After Adam and Eve had been disobedient to God's command, they heard the sound of the Lord walking in the garden, and they hid from Him. God called out to Adam:

> "Where are you? Adam answered, 'I heard you in the garden, and I was afraid because I was naked.' God said, 'Who told you that you were naked?' Have you eaten from the tree that I commanded you not to eat from?" (Genesis 3:8-11).

Deceives People

The psalmist David wrote about sinful hearts when he said:

> "An oracle is in my heart concerning the sinfulness of the wicked: There is no fear of God before his eyes. For in his own eyes he flatters himself too much to detect or hate his sin," (Psalm 36:1-2).

Separates God from Man

The prophet Micah rebuked the leaders for treating the people unfairly, and then expected God to answer their prayers. He said to them:

> "Listen, you leaders of Jacob, you rulers of the house of Israel, should you not know justice, you who hate good and love evil; who tear the skin from my people and the flesh from their bones. Then they will cry out to the Lord, but He will not answer them. At that time, He will hide His face from them because of the evil they have done," (Micah 3:1-2).

Begins with Attitudes and Thoughts

Jesus was teaching on purity when He called the crowd unto Him and said:

> "What comes out of a man is what makes him 'unclean.' For from within, out of men's hearts, come evil thoughts, sexual immorality, theft, murder, adultery, greed, malice, deceit, lewdness, envy, slander, arrogance and folly. All these evils come from inside and make a man 'unclean,'" (Mark 7:20-23).

Prevents People from Receiving Their Blessings

The apostle Paul wrote:

> "Repent, then, and turn to God, so that your sins may be wiped out, that times of refreshing may come from the Lord," (Acts 3:19).

Causes Spiritual Death

The apostle Paul said:

> "Therefore, just as sin entered the world through one man, and death through sin, and in this way death came to all men, because all have sinned," (Romans 5:12).

Is Powerful and Controlling

The apostle Paul wrote:

> "I do not understand what I do. For what I want to do I do not do, but what I hate I do. And if I do what I do not want to do, I agree that the law is good. As it is, it is no longer I myself who do it, but it is sin living in me," (Romans 7:15-17).

SATAN

Satan is the source of all sin and evilness because he is wicked and evil. He is called by many names, but is best known as the "the devil." He is real and is not just the figment of someone's imagination, as is believed by many. The Bible makes it plain that Satan exists and that his main work is to oppose God. Originally, he was an angel of God. But there was a war in heaven where Michael and his angels fought against Satan and his angels. Satan and his angels lost the battle and were kicked out of heaven to earth. Now he leads the whole world astray (Revelation12:7-9). These fallen angels are now called demons, who are really evil spirits, and they are under Satan's control. They are powerful and dangerous. They teach their own doctrines that lead people away from God (1Timothy 4:1).

Because of his defeat, Satan is now God's enemy and the Christian's as well. He works against God through God's own people. He is the author of all evilness and sinfulness in this world. He entices humankind through the cravings of sinful man, the lust of his eyes, and the boasting of what he has and does (1 John 2:16). The apostle Paul taught that the struggles of God's people are not against flesh and blood, but against rulers, authorities, powers of this dark world and against the spiritual forces of evil in the heavenly realms (Ephesians 6:12); these are the powerful evil forces of Satan and his demons. In this age, Satan holds the power of death. But that will not last forever, because Jesus' second coming is ultimately his death. The author of Hebrews wrote:

> "Since the children have flesh and blood, He too shared in their humanity so that by His death He might destroy him who holds the power of death, that is, the devil," (Hebrews 2:14).

God revealed the nature of Satan through His holy Word, so that His people will recognize who and what comes up against them in their spiritual lives. Satan is an intelligent being, so much so that he is clever enough for man not to recognize him for whom he really is, and the havoc he is capable of causing in the lives of people. His main purpose is to rob, steal and kill God's people. The Bible teaches that Satan: is the enemy of God, Prince of this world, a tempter, and a deceiver.

The Enemy of God

God is holy, righteous and just, and cannot tolerate sin. It is Satan's nature to promote sin, because he has been sinning from the beginning (1 John 3:8b). Therefore, he is in direct conflict with God, and works against Him through man. His primary goal is to steal God's people away from Him. He will do anything in his power to get people to follow and worship him, as he did with Jesus when he tempted Him in the desert (Matthew 4:8-9). Scriptures teach that Satan is desirous of blocking God and His plans for His people, and therefore, uses any method necessary to accomplish his goals.

He Tries to Stop the Spread of the Gospel

In explaining the meaning of the parable of the Four Soils, Jesus said:

> "When anyone hears the message about the kingdom and does not understand it, the evil one comes and snatches away what was sown in the heart," (Matthew 13:19).

The apostle Paul said:

> "And even if our gospel is veiled, it is veiled to those who are perishing. The god of this age has blinded the minds of unbelievers, so that they cannot see the light of the gospel of the glory of Christ, who is the image of God," (2 Corinthians 4:3-4).

He Desires Pain and Suffering in God's People

After the first conversation God and Satan had about His servant Job in the Old Testament, Scriptures say:

> "So Satan went out from the presence of the Lord and afflicted Job with painful sore from the soles of his feet to the top of his head," (Job 2:6-7).

When Jesus healed a woman on the Sabbath, He said to the religious leaders:

> "Then should not this woman, whom Satan has kept bound for eighteen long years, be set free" (Luke 13:16).

The apostle Paul wrote in one of his letters:

> "There was given me a thorn in my flesh, a messenger of Satan, to torment me" (2Corinthians 12:7).

The apostle Peter wrote:

> "Be self-controlled and alert. Your enemy the devil, prowls around like a roaring lion looking for someone to devour. Resist him, standing firm in the faith, because you know that your brothers throughout the world are undergoing the same kind of sufferings," (1 Peter 5:8-9).

He Enters into People to Cause Havoc

The chief priests and teachers of the law were looking for a way to get rid of Jesus. The Gospel writer, Luke said:

> "Then Satan entered Judas, one of Jesus' disciples. Judas went to the chief priests and the officers of the temple guard and discussed with them how he might betray Jesus," (Luke 22:2-4).

He is a Schemer

The apostle Paul said:

> "Put on the whole armor of God so that you can take your stand against the devil's schemes," (Ephesians 6:11).

He Confuses the Minds of People

The apostle Paul said:

> "The god of this age has blinded the minds of unbelievers, so they cannot see the light of the gospel of the glory of Christ, who is the image of God," (2 Corinthians 4:4-5).

He Uses Phony Miracles and Signs to Attract People

The apostle Paul said:

> "The coming of the lawless one will be in accordance with the work of Satan, displayed in all kinds of counterfeit miracles, signs and wonders, and in every sort of evil that deceives those that are perishing," (2 Thessalonians 2:9-10).

He Targets Those that are Weak and Non-Alert

The apostle Peter wrote:

> "Be self-controlled and alert. Your enemy, the devil, prowls around like a roaring lion looking for someone to devour," (1 Peter 5:8).

Prince of this World

Satan is the prince of this world (John 12:31). He is responsible for all the evilness that goes on in the world today. The apostle John wrote: "Do not love the world or anything in the world. If anyone loves the world, the love of the Father is not in him," (1John 2:15). Worldliness is not just man's associations and his activities, but is also of the heart. The apostle John said:

> "For everything in the world – the cravings of sinful man (his focus in on gratifying his physical desires); the lust of his eyes (the desire to accumulate possessions); and the boasting of what he has and does (his focus is on power, positions and prestige) comes from the world," (1John 2:16).

Satan has great power, and the whole world is under his influence. Even at that, he will never have an ultimate victory over God's people. Jesus said to His disciples: "In this world you will have trouble, but take heart, I have overcome the world," (John 16:33). But because God created him, God is greater and more powerful than he. From the beginning of Satan's temporary rule on earth, he had limitations set by God.

He Can Only Do What God Allows Him to Do

The Bible teaches that God is fully aware of Satan's activities. It further teaches that He does indeed allow him to work evil among His people, but with limitations. Scriptures in both the Old and New Testaments speak of Satan's limited power. The author of the Book of Job wrote that during a conversation God had with Satan in regards to His servant Job, He said:

> "Very well, then, everything he has is in your hands, but on the man himself do not lay a finger," (Job 1:12).

At another time, The Lord said to Satan, "Very well, then, he is in your hands; but you must spare his life," (Job 2:6).

Jesus said to Peter:

> "Satan has asked to sift you as wheat. But I have prayed for you, Simon, that your faith may not fail," (Luke 22:31-32a).

He Holds the Power of Death

In the Book of Hebrews, it says:

> "Since the children have flesh and blood, He too shared in their humanity so that by His death He might destroy him who holds the power of death, that is, the devil," (Hebrews 2:14).

Tempter

Temptation is one of the methods Satan uses to carry out his evil works. He has the ability to make people think that his way is better than God's way. He is able to make sin seems appealing and, therefore, is able to entice people to sin. With his cunning tricks, he makes "wrong" looks "right," and "bad" looks "good." Since from the beginning of time, he was a tempter, and still is thousands of years later. The Bible records instances of Satan being successful in tempting God's people. It is recorded in the Old Testament by Moses how Satan tempted the first two people God created.

> After being told by God not to eat from the Tree of the Knowledge of Good and Evil, Satan in the form of a serpent tempted Eve to do so. She ate and then gave some to Adam (Genesis 2:15-17; 3:1-6).

David loved the Lord. The Bible says he was "a man after God's own heart." Yet, Satan was successful in tempting him. Scripture says:

> "Satan rose up against Israel and incited David to take a census of Israel," (1 Chronicles 21:1).

Satan tempted Jesus Christ, but was unsuccessful. But being who he is, he did what Satan does to be in control, he continued to work at it. The Gospel writer Luke wrote:

> "Jesus, full of the Holy Spirit, returned from the Jordan and was led by the Spirit in the desert, where for forty days He was tempted by the devil," (Luke 4:1-2).

The apostle Paul said:

> "When we were with you, we kept telling you that we would be persecuted. And it turned out that way, as you well know. For this reason, when I could stand it no longer, I sent to find out about your faith. I was afraid that in some way the tempter might have tempted you and our efforts might have been useless," (I Thessalonians 3:4-5).

He Entices People to Sin

The apostle John recorded:

> "The evening meal was being served, and the devil had already prompted Judas Iscariot to betray Jesus," (John 13:2).

James, the brother of Jesus wrote about the danger of temptations. He said:

"Each one is tempted when, by his own evil desire, he is dragged away and enticed. Then after desire has conceived, it gives birth to sin," (James 1:14).

Deceiver

Satan is deceitful. He masquerades as an angel of light, and his servants masquerade as servants of righteousness (2 Corinthians 11:14). He and his angels are experts in this area. They are masters in deceiving God's people in many ways, but especially in words. The apostle Paul said, "Let no one deceive you with empty words, for because of such things God's wrath comes on those who are disobedient," (Ephesians 5:6). Scriptures reveal Satan as being a great deceiver.

He is the Father of Lies, and there is no Truth in Him

The people were not able to understand what Jesus meant when He spoke to them about being true children of God. In giving His reason for their lack of understanding, He said:

> "Why is my language not clear to you? Because you are unable to hear what I say, you belong to your father, the devil, and you want to carry out your father's desire. He was a murderer from the beginning, not holding to the truth, for there is no truth in him. When he lies, he speaks his native language, for he is a liar and the father of lies," (John 8:42-44).

He Causes People to Lie to God and to Others

> A man named Ananias and his wife, Sapphira, sold a piece of their property. They kept part of the money for themselves and brought the rest and put it at the apostle's feet. Peter said, "Ananias, how is it that Satan

has so filled your heart that you have lied to the holy Spirit and have kept for yourself some of the money you received for the land," (Acts 5:1-3).

He Uses Counterfeit Miracles, Signs and Wonders to Deceive People

The apostle Paul wrote:

> "The coming of the lawless one will be in accordance with the work of Satan, displayed in all kinds of counterfeit miracles, signs and wonders, and in every sort of evil that deceives those who are perishing," (2 Thessalonians 2:9-10a).

He Make People Think more of Themselves than They should

The apostle Paul said to Timothy, in regards to placing young converts in certain offices:

> "He must not be a recent convert, or he may become conceited and fall under the same judgment as the devil," (1Timothy 3:6).

He Distracts People

The apostle Paul wrote:

> "But I am afraid that just as Eve was deceived by the serpent's cunning, your minds may somehow be led astray from your sincere and pure devotion to Christ," (2 Corinthian 11:3).

He Causes People to be Pretenders

Paul said:

> "Such men are false apostles, deceitful workmen masquerading as apostles of Christ. And no wonder, for Satan himself masquerades as an angel of light. It is not surprising, then, if his servants masquerade as servants of righteousness," (2 Corinthians 11:13-15a).

Satan, the great pretender, has been and still is successful in enticing many people to follow him. His primary goal is to try to block God's work through them. They are from all walks of life and cannot be identified by ethnic background, social status or religious persuasion. For whatever reason, many have decided to follow Satan rather than to follow Jesus. John wrote that Jesus said this in regards to Satan's followers, "You belong to your father, the devil, and you want to carry out your father's desires," (John 8:44a). God cannot allow sin to go unchecked in the life of His followers. He has to hold His people accountable for their actions. Man involves himself in many different kinds of sins, all of which God cannot overlook. Solomon, in all of his God-given wisdom wrote, "There are six things the lord hates in people, seven that are detestable to Him, and Satan is responsible for them all. They are:

"Haughty eyes (a proud look),

A lying tongue (a liar),

Hands that shed innocent blood (murderers),

A heart that devises wicked schemes (wicked imaginations),

Feet that are quick to rush into evil (rushing to do evil things),

A false witness who pours out lies (tells premeditated lies),

A man who stirs up dissension among his brothers"
(he keeps confusion in constant motion"), (Proverbs 6:16-19).

Believers struggle with sin every day of their lives. The apostle Paul wrote:

> "I do not understand what I do. For what I want to
> do I do not do, but what I hate I do. As it is, it is no
> longer I myself who do it, but it is sin living in me. I
> know that nothing good lives in me, that is my sinful
> nature. For I have the desire to do what is good, but I
> cannot carry it out," (Romans 7:15, 17-18).

Satan is the "god of this world," but according to Scriptures, he is destined to be destroyed. The Bible says he is going to spend eternity in the lake of burning sulfur (Revelation 20:10). But meanwhile, God's people are living in a world where Satan is an ever present force that is trying to get as many souls as he can.

CHAPTER THREE

Jesus Christ

J esus Christ is God in human form. God took on the flesh of a human being, and came into this world as a man, to live among men. The apostle John said, "The Word became flesh and made His dwelling among us," (John 1:14; 10:30, 38). He is the image of the invisible God. What we cannot see of God because of His invisibility, we can see in Jesus Christ. Because He is God, He has the power and authority to deliver man from sin. He did not come into existence upon His birth into the world, but that He is eternal. The coming of Jesus was spoken of in the Old Testament hundreds of years before His birth. The prophet, Daniel saw Him in one of His visions. He said:

> "In my vision at night I looked, and there before me was one like a Son of Man coming with the clouds of heaven. He approached the Ancient of Days and was led into his presence. He was given authority, glory and sovereign power; all people, nations and men of every language worshiped Him. His dominion is an everlasting dominion that will not pass away, and His kingdom is one that will never be destroyed," (Daniel 7:13-14).

New Testament authors wrote of Jesus being God. The apostle John who was an eyewitness to Jesus and His work said:

"In the beginning was the Word, and the Word was with God, and the Word was God. He was with God in the beginning. Through Him all things were made; without Him nothing was made," (John 1:1-3).

The apostle Paul wrote:

"Jesus is the image of the invisible God, and is the firstborn over all creation. All things were created by Him; things in heaven and on earth, visible and invisible, whether thrones or powers or rulers or authorities, all things were created by Him and for Him. He is before all things, and in Him all things hold together," (Colossians 1:15-17).

Jesus means "The Lord Saves." He came to earth to save men from their sins, because men could not save themselves (Matthew 1:21b). Jesus was born holy and without sin due to His holy birth by a virgin. His birth was prophesied by the prophet Isaiah, saying: "Therefore the Lord Himself will give you a sign: The virgin will be with child and will give birth to a son, and will call Him Emmanuel which means, 'God with us,'" (Isaiah 7:14).The prophet Isaiah also said: "For unto us a child is born, to us a Son is given, and the government will be on His shoulders. And He will be called Wonderful Counselor, Mighty God, Everlasting Father, Prince of Peace," (Isaiah 9:6). These different names help man to understand the nature of Jesus Christ and what He is to be to His people. He will be:

A WONDERFUL COUNSELOR

He will be a wonderful counselor because He will give the best advice, and the needed direction for life. He will guide with love and truth.

A MIGHTY GOD

He will have God's power that will put Him far above all rule and authority, power and dominion, and every title that can be given (Ephesians 1:19-21). He will have power over diseases, sin nature and death. The apostle Paul said, "At the name of Jesus every knee should bow, in heaven and on earth and under the earth, and every tongue confess that Jesus Christ is Lord," (Philippians 2:10-11).

AN EVERLASTING FATHER

He is the Father of eternity. He was at the beginning of time; He is right now, and He will always be. The author of Hebrews states, "Jesus Christ is the same yesterday and today and forever," (Hebrews 13:8).

A PRINCE OF PEACE

He will remove all peace-disturbing factors and secure peace for His people. He said to His disciples; "Peace I leave with you; my peace I give you. I do not give to you as the world gives. Do not let your hearts be troubled and do not be afraid," (John 14:27).

THE SUFFERING SERVANT

He will suffer and die for the sins of the people of the world. He will be despised and rejected by many. He will be pierced for the sins of man and crushed for his iniquities. He will be arrested and beaten, then led like a lamb to the slaughter, and will never utter a word. He will die for the sins of the people, although He had done no wrong. Yet it was the Lord's will that He be crushed and caused to suffer, so that man will have the opportunity to have eternal life (Isaiah 53:2-10).

The prophet Isaiah's prophecy was fulfilled many hundreds of years later when God sent Jesus down from heaven to earth on a mission. He came to save the world from its sins. He left His place in heaven to serve humankind just as was prophesied by Isaiah.

GOD AND JESUS ARE ONE

Jesus was fully God and fully man. God and Jesus being one in the same is the incarnation of Christ. God assumed a human body and came into the world as Jesus, His Son, yet He remained God. The apostle Paul said, "For in Christ all the fullness of the Deity lives in bodily form," (Colossians 2:9). He also said:

> "Who, being in the very nature of God, did not consider equality with God something to be grasped, but made Himself nothing, taking the nature of a servant, being made in human likeness. And being found in appearance as a man, He humbled Himself and became obedient to death, even death on a cross," (Philippians 2:6-8).

Jesus had to reveal to both His disciples and His enemies that He and God are one in the same on more than one occasion. One time the Jews accused Him of being a mere man and of blasphemy, and attempted to stone Him, He said:

> "Why then do you accuse me of blasphemy because I said, 'I am God's Son?' Do not believe me unless I do what my Father does. But if I do, even though you do not believe Me, believe the miracles, that you may know and understand that the Father is in Me, and I in the Father," (John 10:31-38).

When Jesus taught that He was the way to the Father, He said to His disciples:

> "Don't you believe that I am in the Father, and that the Father is in Me? The words I say to you are not just

my own. Rather, it is the Father, living in me, who is doing His work," (John 14:10).

Incarnation

"Incarnation is a theological term for the coming of God's Son into the world as a human being," (Nelson's Illustrated Bible Dictionary). The word itself is not used in the Bible, but Scriptures make clear references to it. New Testament writers recorded that Jesus and God are one in the same. John recorded:

> "The Word became flesh and made His dwelling among us. We have seen His glory, the glory of the One and only, who came from the Father, full of grace and truth," (John 1:14).

Paul, the great apostle, wrote:

> "He is the image of the invisible God, the firstborn over all creation. For by Him all things were created; things in heaven and on earth, visible and invisible, whether thrones or powers or rulers or authorities; all things were created by Him and for Him. He is before all things, and in Him all things hold together," (Colossians 1:15-17).

Jesus' ministry on earth extended over a period of more than three years. During that time, He performed many miracles or signs. He turned water into wine, healed the sick, raised the dead, gave sight to the blind, fed over 5,000 people with two fish and five loaves of bread, walked on water, and calmed a raging sea among many other things.

The Bible teaches that Jesus and others as well, referred to Him using various names or titles that indicated His person, and the special tasks He was ready to perform to help people physically and spiritually. These names and titles were also used to acknowledge Him as more than a mere man, but a man sent by God on a mission to save the world from their sins.

THE SON OF GOD

"When Jesus is presented as the Son of God in the New Testament, two aspects of His person are emphasized: His eternal relation to God as His Father and His perfect revelation of the Father to the human race" (Nelson's Illustrated Bible Dictionary). The Gospel writers spoke of Jesus as being the Son of God before His birth and during His ministry. Before His conception, an angel of God came to Mary, who was a virgin, and told her that she had found favor with God, and that she would give birth to a son and she was to give Him the name Jesus. He said the child would be great and will be called the Son of the Most High. The angel further stated:

> "So the holy one to be born will be called the Son of God," (Luke 1:32-35).

God, the Father referred to Jesus as "His Son." After His baptism, as Jesus was coming up out of the water, he saw heaven being torn open and the Spirit descending on Him like a dove. And a voice came from heaven, saying, "You are my Son, whom I love; with you I am well pleased," (Mark 1:10-11). Another time, Jesus and three of His disciples, Peter, James and John, were in the mountains when His transfiguration took place. The three disciples saw Jesus' face shine like the sun, and his clothes became as white as the light. They heard a voice from the cloud saying:

> "This is my Son whom I love; with Him I am well pleased. Listen to Him," (Matthew 17:1-5).

Jesus referred to Himself as God's Son as He prayed to His Father. He said:

"Father, the time has come. Glorify Your Son, that Your Son may glorify you. For you granted him authority over all people that He might give eternal life to all those you have given Him," (John 17:1-2).

The apostle John recorded:

"Jesus did many other miraculous signs in the presence of His disciples, which are not recorded in this book. But these are written that you may believe that Jesus is the Christ, the Son of God, and that by believing you may have life in His name," (John 20:30-31).

After Jesus' resurrection and ascension back to heaven, He was still referred to as the Son of God. Saul (later called Paul), a Pharisee who hated Christians, recognized Jesus as God's Son soon after his conversion. As a result of his encounter with God, he was baptized and spent some time with the disciples in Damascus. Luke, the Gospel writer said this of Paul:

"At once he began to preach in the synagogues that Jesus is the Son of God," (Acts 9:1-20).

After Jesus' ascension back to heaven, the apostle John said:

"We proclaim to you what we have seen and heard, so that you also may have fellowship with us. And our fellowship is with the Father and with His Son, Jesus Christ," (1 John 1:3).

SON OF DAVID

Jesus is a direct descendant of King David. When He was referred to as the Son of David, it was done in recognition of His earthly lineage to King David. In the Old Testament, the prophet Isaiah wrote of the coming of the Messiah, and that He would be a descendant of David. He said:

> "For to us a child is born, to us a son is given, and the government will be on His shoulders. And He will be called Wonderful Counselor, Mighty God, Everlasting Father, Prince of Peace. Of the increase of His government and peace there will be no end. He will reign on David's throne and over his kingdom, establishing and upholding it with justice and righteousness from that time on and forever," (Isaiah 9:6-7).

Matthew began his Gospel with a record of the genealogy of Jesus Christ that is recorded in Matthew 1:1-16. He wrote:

> "There were fourteen generations in all from Abraham to David, fourteen from David to the exile to Babylon, and fourteen from the exile to the Christ," (Matthew 1:17).

Matthew again recorded that Jesus was acknowledged as the Son of David when he wrote that as Jesus entered into Jerusalem, the people shouted:

> "Hosanna to the Son of David! Blessed is he who comes in the name of the Lord!" (Matthew 21:9).

Other New Testament writers wrote of occasions where others referred to Jesus as the Son of David. Luke recorded that God sent His angel with a message to Mary, stating that:

> "You will be with child and give birth to a son, and you are to give Him the name Jesus. He will be great and will be called the Son of the Most High. The Lord God will give Him the throne of His father David,

and he will reign over the house of Jacob forever; His kingdom will never end," (Luke 1:31-33).

The apostle Peter preached on the Day of Pentecost that David knew that God had promised him that He would place one of his descendants on his throne (Acts 2:29-30).

SON OF MAN

Jesus was both God and man. Being God and coming to earth as a man made Him the Son of God, He was born free of sin and holy. As God's Son, He came to earth on a mission, and that was to save mankind from his sins. "Son of Man" was obviously Jesus' favorite term when He spoke of Himself. He used this terminology throughout the Gospels to describe Himself more than any of the other titles He was given. He used "Son of Man" to identify Himself as a man, yet He was divine. New Testament Scriptures reveal that as a human being, Jesus was able to identify with man's temptations, needs and sufferings because He experienced them. Yet, He did not sin.

He got Hungry

Mark recorded:

> "The next day as they were leaving Bethany, Jesus was hungry," (Mark 11:12).

He got Physically Tired

Luke recorded:

> He was on a boat with his disciples, and as they sailed, He fell asleep (Luke 8:23).

He had Emotions

Matthew recorded that Jesus went through all the towns and villages, teaching, preaching, and healing every disease and sickness. He said when Jesus saw the crowds:

> "He had compassion on them, because they were harassed and helpless, like sheep without a shepherd," (Matthew 9:35-36).

Jesus took some of His disciples with Him to pray in the Garden of Gethsemane. He became distressed and troubled and said to them:

> "My soul is overwhelmed with sorrow to point of death. Stay here and keep watch," (Mark 14:32-34).

As Jesus went into a town, He met a funeral of a young man who was the only child of a widow. When He saw her, His heart went out to her and He said:

> "Don't cry." Without being asked, He touched the coffin and said, "Young man, I say to you, get up," (Luke 7:11-15). The dead man sat up and began to talk and Jesus gave him back to his mother.

When Jesus arrived at Lazarus' home, his sister, Mary went out to meet Him. She fell at His feet and said, "Lord, if you had been here, my brother would not have died." When Jesus saw her crying, and also the others who had come along with her, He was deeply moved in spirit and troubled. He asked:

> "'Where have you laid him?' Then Jesus wept," (John 11:32-35).

Jesus used the term "Son of Man" as He taught His disciples about His mission. Once, He said:

"The Son of Man must suffer many things and be rejected by the elders, chief priests and teachers of the law, and He must be killed and on the third day be raised to life," (Luke 9:21-22; Mark 8:31).

"If anyone is ashamed of Me and My words, The Son of Man will be ashamed of him when he comes in his glory and in the glory of the Father and of the holy angels," (Luke 9:26).

Jesus and His disciples were walking through a field of grain on a Sabbath. The disciples were hungry and began to eat some of the grain. The Pharisees saw them and told them what they were doing was unlawful on the Sabbath. Jesus said to them:

"The Sabbath is made for man, not man for the Sabbath. So the Son of Man is Lord, even of the Sabbath," (Matthew 12:1-2, 8).

Jesus warned His disciples about being prepared for His return. He said:

"You must be ready, because the Son of Man will come at an hour when you do not expect Him," (Luke 12:40).

Stephen, a man full of faith and of the Holy Spirit, and was the first to give his life for the sake of the Gospel, referred to Jesus as the Son of Man. Just before he was stoned to death for his beliefs in Christ, he gazed into heaven and saw the glory of God, then said:

"Look! I see the heavens opened and the Son of Man standing at the right hand of God," (Acts 7:55-56).

THE SAVIOR

Jesus Christ came to earth on a mission; to be the Savior of the world. He was designated by God to save humankind from their sins by dying a horrendous death on the cross for them. The apostle John said, "For God so loved the world, that He gave His One and only Son, that whosoever believes in Him shall not perish but have eternal life," (John 3:16). When God was ready for Jesus' appearance on earth, He sent an angel to tell Joseph who was going to be His earthly father about the birth of the Savior. The angel said:

> "Do not be afraid to take Mary home as your wife, because what is conceived in her is from the Holy Spirit. She will give birth to a son and you are to give him the name Jesus, because he will save his people from their sins," (Matthew 1:20-21).

Jesus knew what His mission was on earth, so He began to teach the people about Himself. As Savior of the world, He made five of His profound "I Am" statements:

"I Am the Bread of Life"

He is the only source of eternal life. He made this proclamation to a group of people who were concerned about Him giving them physical food when He desired spiritual food for them. Jesus declared:

> "I am the bread of life. He who comes to me will never go hungry, and he who believes in Me will never be thirsty. I am the living bread that came down from heaven. If anyone eats of this bread, he will live forever. This bread is my flesh, which I will give for the life of the world," (John 6:22-35).

"I Am the Light of the World"

Jesus is the light the believer needs to keep him from walking in darkness of sin. A woman was brought before Jesus by the Pharisees and the teachers of the law, because they said she was caught in the act of adultery. They wanted to stone her because, according to the Law of Moses, she should be stoned. Jesus said; "If any of you are without sin, let him be the first to throw a stone at her." The people left and Jesus said to her, "Woman, where are they? Has no one condemned you?" She answered, "No one, Sir." Jesus said:

> "Then neither do I condemn you. Go now and leave your life of sin." When He spoke again to the people, He said: "I am the light of the world. Whoever follows Me will never walk in darkness, but will have the light of life," (John 8:3-12).

"I Am the Gate for the Sheep"

It is only through Jesus Christ that man is saved. Jesus painted a picture of a shepherd taking care of His sheep. The sheep knows the shepherd and follows him. They will never follow a stranger because they do not recognize his voice. When Jesus talked about the shepherd and the sheep, the people did not understand what He was telling them. Then Jesus said:

> "I tell you the truth; I am the gate for the sheep. All who ever came before me were thieves and robbers, but the sheep did not listen to them. I am the gate; whoever enters through Me will be saved," (John 10:1-9).

"I Am the Good Shepherd"

He loves His people, and is committed to them. He took it another step further in this picture that He painted to show the love He has for His followers by saying:

> "I am the good shepherd. I know My sheep and My sheep know Me, just as the father knows Me and I know the Father, and I lay down My life for the sheep. I have other sheep that are not of this sheep pen. I must bring them also. They too will listen to my voice, and there shall be one flock and one Shepherd," (John 10:14-16).

"I Am the Resurrection and the Life"

Next, He declared, "I Am the Resurrection and the Life," meaning His followers will die, but will live again. A friend of Jesus' had been dead and buried for four days before Jesus arrived. When the dead man's sister saw Him coming, she went out to meet Him and said, "Lord, if you had been here, my brother would not have died." Jesus told her that her brother will rise again. She answered by saying; "I know he will rise again in the resurrection at the last day," Jesus said to her:

> "I am the resurrection and the life. He who believes in me will live, even though he dies, and whoever lives and believes in me will never die," (John 11:17-25).

"I Am the Way, the Truth, and the Life"

He is the only way to the Father because He alone is from the Father. After Jesus and the disciples had the Last Supper together, He told them He would be with them only a little while longer, and where He was going they could not follow Him now, but that He would come back and take them to be with Him. He said to them, "You will know the way to the place where I am going." Thomas said to Him, "Lord, we don't know where you are going, so how can we know the way?" Jesus answered:

> "I am the way, and the truth and the life. No one comes to the Father except through Me," (John 14:1-6)

Scripture writers in the New Testament wrote of Jesus being Savior at birth, before His ministry began, and during His ministry. Luke recorded that as the shepherds were watching over their flock one night, an angel of the Lord appeared to them, and said:

> "Do not be afraid, I bring you good news of great joy that will be for all the people. Today in the town of David a Savior has been born to you; He is Christ, the Lord," (Luke 2:5-11).

When John the Baptist, looked up and saw Jesus coming toward him, he said:

> "Look, the Lamb of God, who takes away the sin of the world," (John 1:29).

The apostle John wrote:

> "God did not send His Son into the world to condemn the world, but to save the world through Him," (John 3:17).

While teaching James and John about serving others, Jesus referred to Himself as Savior when He said:

> "Whoever wants to be first must be slave of all. For even the Son of Man did not come to be served, but

to serve, and to give His life as a ransom for many," (Matthew 20:20-28; Mark 10:35-45).

Jesus' coming into the world as Savior as He did, and when He did was not an afterthought of God. Old Testament prophets prophesied of His birth hundreds of years before His actual birth. Bible scholars say that Jesus was being referred to in the beginning in Genesis 3:15 when God said to the serpent: "And I will put enmity between you and the woman, and between your offspring and hers; He will crush your head, and you will strike His heel." God is the source of salvation, and Jesus Christ is Savior for all of humankind.

THE MESSIAH/CHRIST

Messiah/Christ means the Anointed One, and is the name for Jesus which shows that He was empowered by God's Spirit to deliver His people from their sins. "In Christian thought, the term Messiah refers to Jesus' role as a spiritual deliverer, setting His people free from sin and death," (Nelson's Illustrated Bible Dictionary). The Jewish people in Bible days were looking for a political leader who would deliver them from Roman rule. When Jesus made His appearance and began His ministry, He did not measure up to the expectations of the Jews. He was rejected by most of them because they could not believe that the son of a carpenter was the long-awaited Messiah. Although, many Jews had trouble believing in Him, some did. In speaking to those who believed in Him, He said to them, "And you shall know the truth and the truth shall make you free," (John 8:32 NKJV). New Testament writers referred to Him as the Christ. The apostle John said:

> "Jesus did many other miraculous signs in the presence of His disciples, which are not recorded in this book. But that these are written so that man may believe that Jesus is the Christ, the Son of the God, and that

by believing one may have life in his name," (John 20:30-31).

After Jesus' death and resurrection, His followers still maintained that He is the Christ. During Peter's address on the Day of Pentecost, he spoke on the resurrection of Jesus, saying:

> "God has made this Jesus, whom you crucified, both Lord and Christ," (Acts 2:36).

After being jailed, the apostles Peter and John continued in their ministry of preaching and teaching. Luke recorded:

> "Day after day, in the temple courts and from house to house, they continued teaching and proclaiming the good news that Jesus is the Christ," (Act 5:42).

As Paul went on his missionary journeys, setting up the early Christian churches and establishing the foundation of the Christian faith, he proclaimed Jesus as the Christ. He went into the synagogue and preached to the people from the Scriptures, explaining and proving that the Christ had to suffer and rise from the dead. He said:

> "This Jesus I am proclaiming to you is the Christ," (Acts 17:1-3).

LORD

When Jesus is referred to as Lord, it indicates His mighty powers. This title was used to give some insight into His loving, kind, just and compassionate nature. Jesus referred to Himself as Lord when He was teaching the people that what they say must reflect what they do when He said:"Not everyone who says to me, 'Lord, Lord,' will enter the kingdom of heaven, but only he who does the will of My Father who is in heaven," (Matthew 7:21).

It was during the Passover Feast that He showed His disciples the extent of His love for them. He got up from the evening meal, and began to teach His disciples a lesson on humility. He wrapped a towel around His waist and began to wash their feet. When He finished, He said:

> "You call me 'Teacher' and 'Lord,' and rightly so, for that is what I am. Now that I, your Lord and Teacher, have washed your feet, you also should wash one another's feet. I have set an example that you should do as I have done for you," (John 13: 13-15).

Many others saw Jesus as "Lord," and referred to Him as such when He showed compassion to those in need. Others acknowledged His power over physical and spiritual death. While in one town, large crowds followed Him as He came down from the mountainside. A man with leprosy approached Him and said:

> "Lord, if you are willing, you can make me clean." Jesus reached out His hand and touched the man, then said, "I am willing. Be clean!" The man was instantly healed of leprosy. (Matthew 8:1-4; Luke 5:12-13).

After Jesus healed the centurion's servant, a large crowd followed after Him to another town. Upon approaching the town gate, he met a funeral of a young man who was the only child of a widow. Luke recorded:

> "When the Lord saw her, His heart went out to her and He said, 'don't cry.' Without being asked, He touched the coffin and said, "Young man, I say to you, get up!" The dead man sat up and began to talk and Jesus gave him back to his mother (Luke 7:11-15).

After Jesus' death, burial, and resurrection, those who loved Him still believed Him to be Lord. As the disciples left Jesus' empty tomb and went back home, Mary Magdalene stood outside the tomb crying. She bent down to look inside the tomb and saw two angels seated where Jesus' body had been. They asked her what she was crying about. She replied:

> "They have taken my Lord away, and I don't know where they have put Him," (John 20:11-13).

The apostle Peter spoke of Jesus as Lord after His ascension back to heaven. In his address on the Day of Pentecost, Peter told the crowd:

> "God has made this Jesus, whom you crucified, both Lord and Christ," (Acts 2:36).

The apostle Paul referred to Jesus as Lord in his teaching on righteousness. He said:

> "For the wages of sin is death, but the gift of God is eternal life in Christ Jesus our Lord," (Romans 6:23).

PREACHER

As a preacher, Jesus' desire was for His followers to learn of God's Words and live their lives according to His teachings. Preaching was a part of His threefold ministry, which consisted of preaching, teaching and healing. Matthew, recorded that, "From that time on Jesus began to preach, 'Repent, for the kingdom of heaven is near,'" (Matthew 4:17). The Bible says it was customary for Jesus to preach as He traveled from city to city.

Matthew recorded:

> "He went throughout Galilee teaching in their synagogues, preaching the good news of the kingdom

and healing every disease and sickness among the people," (Matthew 4:23).

Mark recorded that Jesus said to His disciples:

> "Let us go somewhere else, to the nearby villages, so I can preach there also. That is why I have come," (Mark 1:38).

Jesus went back to Nazareth, His hometown, and on the Sabbath He went into the synagogue, as was His custom. He was handed the scroll of Isaiah and when He found the place, He proceeded to read:

> "The Spirit of the Lord is on me, because He has anointed me to preach good news to the poor. He has sent me to proclaim freedom for the prisoners and recovery of sight for the blind, to release the oppressed, to proclaim the year of the Lord's favor," (Luke 4:16-19).

He also said:

> "I must preach the good news of the kingdom of God to the other towns also, because that is why I was sent," (Luke 4:43).

Jesus' longest sermon was taught on a mountainside. This sermon is now referred to as "The Sermon on the Mount" where Jesus preached to everyone who gathered around Him to hear His words. His message was entirely different from their previous teachings because the primary focus was on conduct suitable for the Kingdom of God (Matthew 5:1-7:27).

The Sermon on the Mount

In this Sermon, Jesus taught what is referred to today as "The Beatitudes" to His disciples and other followers. These are Jesus' standards of conduct for believers. The purpose of the teaching was to change the thinking of those who believed in Him and had received His Word.

The Beatitudes

The Scriptures in Matthew 5:3-11, known as "The Beatitudes," are not something that a person does but, instead, are inner spiritual qualities that will direct his life and make him pleasing in the sight of God. In this setting, Jesus informed the disciples and the crowds that followed Him that there are spiritual blessings in living a life led by spiritual attitudes. The Beatitudes are:

> "Blessed are the poor in spirit," (those who recognize that they need God's divine assistance in their lives). *The blessing: They will be a part of the kingdom of heaven.*

> "Blessed are those who mourn," (those who express sincere sorrow over a loss, whether it is spiritual or material). *The blessing: They will be forgiven and, therefore, comforted by God's love.*

> "Blessed are the meek," (those that show humility by putting others before themselves, and especially making God first in their lives). *The blessing: They will inherit everything God has promised them.*

"Blessed are those who hunger and thirst for righteousness," (those who have a passion for the righteousness of God).
The blessing: Their lives will reflect God's standards of holiness.

"Blessed are the merciful," (those who show kindness, compassion and forgiveness to others in need).
The blessing: They will be shown kindness, compassion and forgiveness by God and others.

"Blessed are the pure in heart," (those who are cleansed, and seek to be continuously cleansed of sin and filled with the Holy Spirit).
The blessing: They will one day see God's face.

"Blessed are the peacemakers," (those who have peace with God and seek to keep peace among others).
The blessing: They will be called children of God.

"Blessed are those who are persecuted because of righteousness," (those who are willing to live a life according to God's principles, even if they are mistreated for their faith in Him).
The blessing: They too will be a part of the kingdom of heaven.

(Matthew 5:1-11).

In His Sermon on the Mount, Jesus taught many other principles and doctrines that were in total opposition to what the Jewish teachers of the law had taught the people. He taught that the standards that had been set in place for interacting with one another, and some religious practices, were not of God. They were just lots of rules that they had to follow, but had nothing to do with the heart. Jesus began to teach them God's ways. Many of the subject areas began with, "You have heard it was said, or it has been said." Jesus adds to that, "But I tell you." After that statement, Jesus states His truths.

Making a Difference

Jesus wanted his followers to realize that as His followers, they need to make a positive difference in the world. He wanted them to live lives that pointed men toward Him. He said to them:

> "You are the salt of the earth. But if the salt loses its saltiness, how can it made salty again? It is no longer good for anything, except be thrown out and trampled by men." He also let them know that as His disciples, they should stand out as lights in darkness. Their lifestyles should lead men to Christ when He said, "Let your lights shine before men, that they may see your good deeds and praise your Father in heaven," (Matthew 5:13-16).

God's Law

God gave the Laws in the Old Testament for His people to live by, namely The Ten Commandments. In this law, the will of God is revealed. Many other laws were given to the people by the religious leaders that were not of God. As Jesus taught, it was necessary for Him to let His followers know that He did not come to get rid of God's Laws, but had to speak against the many other man-made rules that had been attached and had no spiritual value. He wanted the people to know that they were expected to honor and obey God's commands, and will be rewarded for doing so. He said to them:

> "Do not think that I have come to abolish the Law or the Prophets; I have not come to abolish them but

to fulfill them. I tell you the truth, until heaven and earth disappear, not the smallest letter, not the least stroke of a pen will by any means disappear from the Law until everything is accomplished. Anyone who breaks one of the least of these commandments and teaches others to do the same will be called the least in the kingdom of heaven, but whoever practices and teaches these commands will be called great in the kingdom of heaven. For I tell you that unless your righteousness surpasses that of the Pharisees and teachers of the law, you will certainly not enter the kingdom of heaven," (Matthew 5:17-20).

Anger

Anger is a natural emotion due to our sinful nature, but it is not of God. It does not bring about righteous character that God is looking for in His people. No matter what happens, man must be able to control his anger. It must not dictate his actions. James, the brother of Jesus wrote, "Everyone should be quick to listen, slow to speak and slow to become angry, for a man's anger does not bring about the righteous life that God desires," (James 1:19-20).
Jesus said to His followers:

> "I tell you that anyone who is angry with his brother will be subject to judgment," (Matthew 5:22a).

Lust

Lust is a sinful desire. Most people look at it as sexual only, but it can be an overly zealous or greedy desire for almost anything. In this context, Jesus had to clarify what they had been taught about adultery and lust. He said:

"You have heard that it was said, 'Do not commit adultery.' But I tell you that anyone who looks at a woman lustfully has already committed adultery with her in his heart," (Matthew 5:27-28).

Divorce

God instituted marriage and meant it to be permanent. Moses was the first religious leader who permitted some sort of a divorce law. When Jesus was questioned about that, He said, "Moses permitted you to divorce your wives because your hearts were hard," (Matthew 19:7-8).

To prove that divorce was not a part of God's plans for married couples, Jesus said that when a man is united with his wife, the two will become one flesh. Since they are of one flesh, He added that what God joined together, let no man separate (Mark 10:7-9). Jesus gave the only reason for divorce when He said:

"But I tell you anyone who divorces his wife, except for marital unfaithfulness, causes her to become an adulteress, and anyone who marries the divorced woman commits adultery," (Matthew 5:32).

Making Oaths

The people did not need to make oaths or vows. They just simply needed to tell the truth. They had been taught that they should not break their oaths, but keep the ones they made to the Lord. Jesus taught that people should not take vows or oaths, just tell the truth at all times. He said:

"Do not swear at all: either by heaven, for it is God's throne; or by the earth, for it is His footstool; or by Jerusalem, for it is the city of the Great king. And do not swear by your head, for you cannot make even one hair white or black. Simply let your 'Yes' be 'Yes,' and your 'No,' 'No'; anything beyond this comes from the evil one," (Matthew 5:33-37).

Retaliation

God does not want His people to retaliate or "get even" with someone who has committed a wrong against them. Instead, He desires that man pray for the one who wronged him. The expression, "An eye for an eye, and a tooth for a tooth," had been interpreted to mean getting even with someone for what they had done to you. Jesus cleared up this misconception by telling His followers:

> "You have heard that it was said, 'An eye for an eye, and tooth for a tooth.' But I tell you. Do not resist an evil person. If someone strikes you on the right cheek, turn to him the other one also. And if someone wants to sue you and take your tunic, let him have your cloak as well. If someone forces you to go one mile, go with him two miles. Give to the one who asks you, and do not turn away from the one who wants to borrow from you," (Matthew 5:38-42).

Loving Enemies

The people had been taught to love their neighbors and hate their enemies, but Jesus taught them to love their enemies too. He said:

> "Love your enemies and pray for those who persecute you, that you may be sons of your Father in heaven. He causes His sun to rise on the evil and good, and sends rain on the righteous and the unrighteous," (Matthew 5:43-45).

Giving to the Needy

Jesus said, "The poor you will always have with you," (Matthew 26:11). God expects those whom He has blessed to have more, to help those who have less. When giving to the poor, it should be done privately and sincerely, as Jesus was concerned with the motive for giving. The act of giving to the needy should be done out of compassion, and not for recognition nor with the thought of being paid back. He said:

> "Be careful not to do your acts of righteousness before men, to be seen by them. If you do, you will have no reward from your Father in heaven. So when you give to the needy, do not announce it with trumpets, as the hypocrites do in the synagogues and on the streets, to be honored by men. I tell you the truth; they have received their reward in full. But when you give to the needy, do not let your left hand know what your right hand is doing, so that our giving may be in secret. Then your Father, who sees what is done in secret, will reward you," (Matthew 6:1-4).

Prayer

There is place for public prayer in the life of the believer, but in this session, Jesus addresses private prayer. When personal prayer is offered to God, it should be private and come from a sincere heart. Personal prayers do not have to be heard by others. They do not need to be long and dragged out because God knows what you need before you ask Him for it. He said to His followers:

> "And when you pray, do not be like the hypocrites, for they love to pray standing in the synagogues and on the street corners to be seen by men. I tell you the truth; they have received their reward in full. But

when you pray, go into your room, close the door and pray to your Father, who is unseen. Then your Father who sees what is done in secret, will reward you. And when you pray, do not keep on babbling like pagans for they think they will be heard because of their many words. Do not be like them, for your Father knows what you need before you ask Him," (Matthew 5:5-8).

After teaching them about Prayer, Jesus taught them how to pray. He said to them: "This then is how you should pray:

"Our Father in heaven, hallowed be your name (Acknowledging God for who He is.),

Your kingdom come, your will be done on earth as it is in heaven (praying for God's work in this world.),

Give us today our daily bread (praying for daily needs.),

Forgive us our debts, as we also have forgiven our debtors (asking for forgiveness, as we forgive others.),

And lead us not into temptation, but deliver us from the evil one,"(praying for help in our daily struggles.) (Matthew 6:9-13).

Today, in the Christian world, this prayer is referred to as "The Lord's Prayer." But it is really a model prayer, and is to be used as a pattern in the Christian's daily prayers to God. In it, Jesus let them know how they should pray.

Fasting

Fasting is a religious practice where people deprive themselves of food and spend time in prayer. This is private time spent between God and man. Man humbles himself before God by letting Him know he is depending on Him for his needs to be met, and other prayers to be answered. The outward appearance should not indicate to others that someone is fasting. Jesus taught against hypocrisy in regards to fasting. He said:

> "When you fast, do not look somber as the hypocrites do, for they disfigure their faces to show men they are fasting. I tell you the truth; they have received their reward in full. But when you fast, put oil on your head and wash your face, so that it will not be obvious to men that you are fasting, but only to your Father, who is unseen; and your Father who sees what is done in secret, will reward you," (Matthew 6:16-18).

Money

God expects His people to be good stewards over the possessions He has blessed them with, and money is one of them. It is good to have money, but it is even better to know how to use it wisely; such as helping the poor and supporting the church by paying tithes as God has commanded. Money should not be spent foolishly, nor should it be kept to be boasted about. Jesus knew that man could make his money his god, so He taught:

> "Do not store up for yourselves treasures on earth. For where your treasure is, there your heart will be also." He added that, "No one can serve two masters. Either he will hate the one and love the other, or he will be devoted to the one and despise the other. You cannot serve both God and money," (Matthew 6:19-24).

Worrying

Worrying is not of God. It shows a lack of faith in Him. Jesus taught that God knows man's every need, so instead of worrying, Jesus said, "Seek first His kingdom and His righteousness and all things will be given to you as well," (Matthew 6:33). Life is too short for man to spend time worrying about things he has no control over. God, the Creator is in control of all things. So instead of worrying, just trust God. Jesus said:

> "Do not worry about your life, what you eat or drink; or about your body, or what you will wear. Is not life more important than food, and the body more important than clothes?" Then He uses the birds of the air as an example because they are not able to store up food for themselves, but God provides for them. Then He asks the question, "Are you not much more valuable than they? Who of you by worrying can add a single hour to your life?" He went on to say, "Why do you worry about clothes?" He told them that the lilies of the field grow beautifully, and they are not able to provide for themselves. Surely, if God provides for them, He will clothe His people. Finally, He said, "Therefore do not worry about tomorrow, for tomorrow will worry about itself. Each day has enough trouble of its own," (Matthew 6:25-34).

Being Critical of Others

Before judging others, we must first judge ourselves and then be willing to forgive others. Constructive criticism is good and is meant to be helpful. Destructive criticism is meant to tear others down, and it is not of God. Jesus said:

"Do not judge, or you too will be judged. For in the same way you judge others, you will be judged, and with the measure you use, it will be measured to you. Why do you look at the speck of sawdust in your brother's eye and pay no attention to the plank in your own eye?" (Matthew 7:1-3).

Trusting in God

God is a faithful God, and wants His people to put their faith and trust in Him and His Word. The psalmist wrote, "Trust in the Lord with all your heart and lean not to your own understanding," (Psalm 3:5). Man does not have to understand it all, but just needs to trust God, knowing that He has all the answers. God told Paul, "My grace is sufficient for you, for my power is made perfect in weakness," (2 Corinthians 12:9a). Even when the "bad" seems to be getting worse, God delights in man's trust in Him that He is there for him and his prayers will be answered. In teaching about trusting God, Jesus said:

"Ask and it will be given to you; seek and you will find; knock and the door will be opened to you. For everyone who asks receives; he who seeks, finds; and to him who knocks, the door will be opened," (Matthew 7:7-8).

The Way to Heaven

There is only one way to get to heaven, and that is to believe in the Lord Jesus Christ, that He died for the sins of the world and was resurrected on the third day. Jesus Himself said, "I am the way and the truth and the life. No one comes to the Father except through me," (John 14:6). In Jesus' teachings about the way to heaven, He used the example of a gate when He said:

"Enter through the narrow gate. For wide is the gate and broad is the road that leads to destruction, and many enter through it. But small is the gate and narrow the road that leads to life, and only a few find it," (Matthew 7:13-14).

Fruit in the Lives of People

A good tree cannot bear bad fruit, and a bad tree cannot bear good fruit, and so it is in the lives of people. Jesus was very concerned with false teachers in His days. Their teachings, neither their behavior matched up to God's principles and doctrines. Because of this, Jesus said:

"Watch out for false prophets. They come to you in sheep's clothing, but inwardly they are ferocious wolves. By their fruit you will recognize them. Do people pick grapes from thorn bushes, or figs from thistles? Likewise, every good tree bears good fruit, but a bad tree bears bad fruit. A good tree cannot bear bad fruit, and a bad tree cannot bear good fruit. Every tree that does not bear good fruit is cut down and thrown into the fire. Thus, by their fruit you will recognize them," (Matthew 7:15-20).

Entering into the Kingdom of God

Not everyone who calls on the name of Jesus will get into heaven. One must accept Jesus Christ as Lord and Savior, and be obedient to His Words. Many will think they will have earned the right to get into heaven because they have done good things for others, attended church and served on a ministry, and even has the prominent family name in the church. Jesus said:

"Not everyone who says to me, 'Lord, Lord' will enter the kingdom of heaven, but only he who does the will of my Father who is in heaven. Many will say to me on that day, 'Lord, Lord, did we not prophesy in your name and in your name, drive out demons and perform many miracles?' Then I will tell them plainly, 'I never knew you. Get away from me you evildoers,'" (Matthew 7:21-23).

Jesus' teachings were on the kingdom of God. He wanted His listeners to believe in Him, and that His teachings would remain in their hearts.

TEACHER

Jesus began his ministry after His baptism, His temptations by Satan in the wilderness, and the choosing of some of his disciples. He went throughout Galilee, teaching in their synagogues, preaching the good news of the kingdom, and healing every disease and sickness among the people. He taught every opportunity he got and the people were amazed at His teachings because His messages were spoken with authority (Luke 4:32). News of His ministry spread throughout the area. The teaching part of His ministry showed His desire for the understanding of God's Word for the people. He taught them God's principles and doctrines so that they will know His will and way.

Jesus had compassion on a crowd that had followed Him to another town on foot. He saw them as sheep without a shepherd, so He began teaching them many things (Mark 6:30-34). Jesus referred to Himself as "Teacher" while teaching His disciples. He taught against the religious leaders and their practices when He said:

"You must obey them and do everything they tell you. But do not do what they do, for they do not practice what they preach. Everything they do is for man to see. You are not to be called 'Rabbi,' for you have only one Master and you are all brothers. Nor are you to be

called 'teacher,' for you have one Teacher, the Christ,"
(Matthew 23:1-10).

John recorded that Jesus had attended a Feast, and it was not until
halfway through the Feast did He go up to the temple courts and
began to teach. The Jews were amazed and asked, "How did this man
get such learning without having studied?" Jesus answered:

> "My teaching is not my own. It comes from Him who
> sent me. If anyone chooses to do God's will, he will
> find out whether my teaching comes from God or
> whether I speak on my own," (John 7:14-17).

Even the Pharisees referred to Jesus as Teacher as they observed Him
at work. They felt threatened by His teachings, so they asked Him
questions on important issues to the Jews to test Him. They asked the
questions, and He answered each question in His own way. They said:

> "Teacher, we know you are a man of integrity. You
> aren't swayed by men because you pay no attention
> to who they are; but you teach the way of God in
> accordance with the truth. Is it right to pay taxes to
> Caesar or not? Should we pay or shouldn't we? Jesus
> answered, give to Caesar what is Caesar's and give to
> God what is God's," Matthew 22:15-22; Mark 12:13-
> 17; Luke 20:20-26).

> "Teacher, which is the greatest commandment in the
> law?" Jesus replied, "Love the Lord your God with
> all your heart and with all your soul and with all your
> mind. This is the first and greatest commandment.
> And the second is like it: Love your neighbor as
> yourself," (Matthew 22:35-39; Mark 12:28-34).

Nicodemus, a Pharisee and a member of the Jewish ruling council, came to Jesus at night for a different reason. He said to Jesus:

> "Rabbi (teacher), we know you are a teacher who has come from God. For no one could perform the miraculous signs you are doing if God were not with him," (John 3:1-2).

It was very early in Jesus' ministry that He went throughout Galilee, teaching in their synagogues, preaching and healing. News about His good works spread all over the area, and large crowds followed Him (Matthew 4:23b). Many of Jesus' teachings to large groups were done in the form of parables. A parable is an earthly story with a heavenly meaning.

Parables

In these lessons, Jesus always used something familiar to teach new spiritual truths. This method of teaching was designed to help the people listen, so they can figure out and understand the true meaning of what Jesus was saying. Throughout the Gospels, as He taught, He used parables to explain spiritual truths such as:

The Kingdom of Heaven/The Kingdom of God

"Jesus traveled about from one town and village to another, proclaiming the good news of the Kingdom of God," (Luke 8:1a). These are some of the parables He used to teach lessons on the kingdom of heaven/the kingdom of God.

The Four Soils

A farmer went out to sow his seeds. As he was scattering them, some fell along the path, and the birds came and ate it up. Some fell on rocky places, where it did not have much soil. It sprang up quickly because the soil was shallow. But when the sun came up, the plants were scorched, and they withered because they had no root. Other seeds fell among thorns, which grew up and choked the plants. Still other seeds fell on good soil, where it produced a crop (Matthew 13:3-23; Mark 4:2-25; Luke 8:4-15).

The spiritual truth of this parable is that God's Word is spoken, but is received by people in different ways. Sometimes, it falls on deaf ears and therefore is rejected; sometimes it is received, but stays with them for a short time; and sometime it falls on ears that are ready to accept it and become productive citizens in the Kingdom of God.

The Wheat and the Tare

Jesus said, "The kingdom of heaven is like a man who sowed good seed in his field." Now while everyone was sleeping, his enemy came and sowed weed among his good seeds. As the wheat grew and sprouted, the weed grew along with it. The owner's servant wanted to know where the weeds came from since the owner planted good seed. He asked if they should pull up the weeds. The owner did not allow him to because he might damage the root of the wheat. He told him to let them grow together until the harvest. At that time, he will instruct them to find the weeds, tie them in bundles and burn them, then bring the wheat to his barn (Matthew 13:24-30).

The spiritual truth of this parable is that the weeds growing in with the wheat represents God's people living in the world side by side with people of the world. It is not man's place to judge anyone. In the end, God will separate the good from the evil.

The Unforgiving Debtor

Jesus said, "The kingdom of Heaven is like a king who wanted to settle accounts with his servants." As he began the settlement, a man came before him who owed him a very large sum of money, but was not able to pay him. He ordered that the man, his wife, children and all he had be sold to repay him. The servant fell to his knees before the king and told him to be patient with him, and that he would pay back everything. His master took pity on him and canceled the debt. When the servant went out, he found one of his fellow servants who owed him much less than he owed his master. He grabbed him, choked him and demanded that he pay back the money he owed him. His fellow servant said the same thing to him as he had said to the master, "Be patient with me, and I will pay you back." He did not accept that, but instead had the man thrown into prison until he could pay the money back. The other servants saw what happened. They went back and told the master what they had seen. Then the master called the servant in and said to him, "You wicked servant, I canceled all that debt of yours because you begged me to. Shouldn't you have had mercy on your fellow servant just as I had on you?" Then out of anger, the master turned him over to the jailers to be tortured until he could pay back all he owed (Matthew 18:23-34).

The spiritual truth to this parable is that man should do unto others as he would have them do unto him. Also, if you want to be forgiven, you must be able to forgive those who sin against you.

Christ's Return

In teaching of His return, Jesus used this parables to show that no man knows when His second coming will be, and therefore must stay alert, be obedient and prepared for his return at anytime:

The Ten Bridesmaids

Jesus said in this parable, "At that time the kingdom of heaven will be like ten virgins who took their lamps out to meet the bridegroom. Five of them were foolish and five were wise. The foolish ones took their lamps but did not take any oil with them. The wise ones took oil in jars, along with their lamps." He continued by saying that the bridegroom was late coming, and that the ten virgins fell asleep, and while they were sleeping, all the lamps went out. At midnight the call was made that the bridegroom had arrived, and for all to come out and meet him. The ten virgins got up and started to trim their lamps. The five foolish ones realizing they had no oil for their lamps asked the wise ones for some of their oil. The wise ones refused them, and they had to go out and buy some. When they returned, the bridegroom was there and the five wise virgins had gone in with the bridegroom into the banquet, and the doors were locked. They asked to be let in but were refused (Matthew 25:1-13).

The spiritual truth of this parable is that God's people must live their lives every day anticipating the return of Jesus Christ. They must live in obedience to God's Word as much as possible because nobody knows the day or hour of His return.

God's Love

In teaching of God's love for His people, Jesus used these parables to show that God loves everybody and it is His desire that everyone be saved, and not one of them lost. He expressed God's love for His people using these parables:

The Lost Sheep

The tax collectors and "sinners" were all gathered around Jesus to hear His teachings. The Pharisees and teachers of the law complained about who Jesus was keeping company with. When Jesus heard them complaining, He told a parable by asking them if one of them had one hundred sheep and one got lost, would he leave the ninety-nine in the open country and go look for the lost sheep until he finds it. After he finds it, and joyfully bring it back home, then would he call his friends and neighbors together to rejoice with him because he had found his lost sheep? Then Jesus said to them, "I tell you that in the same way there will be more rejoicing in heaven over one sinner who repents than over ninety-nine persons who do not need to repent,"(Luke 15:1-7).

The spiritual truth of this parable is that God loves man so much that He gives him more than one chance to come to Him, and when he is saved, heaven rejoices.

The Lost Son

This time Jesus told a parable about a man who had two sons. The younger one asked for his part of the estate. The father divided his property between the two sons. The younger son went off and squandered his wealth in wild living. There came a famine in the land, and he had no food or money. He had to take a job feeding pigs. He got so hungry that he thought about eating some of the food he was feeding the pigs. When he came to his senses, he decided to go back home, and ask his father's forgiveness. So he got up and started home, as he approached the father's home, the father saw him coming, and was filled with compassion for him. He ran to him, and threw his arms around him and kissed him. The son said, "Father, I have sinned against heaven and against you. I am no longer worthy to be called your son." The father ordered the best robe for his son, along with a ring for his finger and sandals for his feet. They prepared a feast to celebrate the son's homecoming. The father said, "For this son of mine was dead and is alive again; he was lost and is found." The older brother complained about the treatment of his brother. The father said, "My son, you are always with me, and everything I have is yours. We have to celebrate and be glad, because this brother of yours was dead and is alive again. He was lost and is found," (Luke 15:11-31).

The spiritual truth of this parable is that God has unconditional love for humankind, and He wants them to repent of their sins and turn back to Him.

Humility

In these parables, Jesus taught that anyone who exalts himself will be humbled, and he who humbles himself will be exalted. He told these parables about people acting as if they are better than everyone else when God sees all men as equals:

Seeking Honor

Some people were invited to a wedding feast. Jesus noticed how they chose the places of honor at a table. He told them as invited guests, they do not take the place of honor because someone more distinguished than they may have been invited, and they might be asked to move. They, being humiliated, will have to take the least important place. But what they should do is take the lowest place, and then be asked to move to a better place, where they will be honored in the presence of all the guests. And then He said, "For everyone who exalts himself will be humbled, and he who humbles himself will be exalted," (Luke 14:7-11).

The spiritual truth of this parable is that God's people should not think too highly of themselves, and should put others above themselves.

Two Men Prayed

Jesus gave this parable of someone who is confident of their own righteousness and looked down on everybody else. Two men went up to the temple to pray. One was a Pharisee who prayed about himself. He thanked God that he was not like the other men: robbers, evildoers, and adulterers, and even a tax collector. He said that he fasts twice a week, and gives a tenth of what he has. The second man, a tax collector stood at a distance. He did not look up to heaven, but said, "God, have mercy on me, a sinner." Jesus said, "I tell you that this man, rather than the other, went home justified before God. For everyone who exalts himself will be humbled, and he who humbles himself will be exalted," (Luke18:9-14).

The spiritual truth to this parable is that man should not be self-righteous and proud, but humble.

Neighbors

There are needy people close by everywhere, and whenever and wherever possible, it is expected of the believer to meet their needs. In this parable, Jesus used two men of two different nations of people to show that any person you come in close contact with is your neighbor.

The Good Samaritan

An expert in the law told Jesus what the law said about how to inherit eternal life when he said, "Love the Lord your God with all your heart and with all your soul and with all your strength and with all your mind, and love your neighbor as yourself." Jesus told the man that he was correct, and if he did that he would live. Because the man wanted to justify himself, he said, "And who is my neighbor?" Then Jesus told this parable about a Jewish man who was coming down from Jerusalem to Jericho when he met some men who robbed him, took his clothes, beat him and left him half dead. A priest (a Jew) passed by and saw him in that condition, but did not stop to help him. Another person from a different Jewish tribe saw the man and did what the priest did. Next, the Samaritan (a non-Jew) traveled that same road and saw the man. He went over to help him. He bandaged his wound, put the man on his donkey and took him to an inn and took care of him. The next day, he gave the innkeeper two silver coins to take care of the man until he returns, and upon his arrival, he would reimburse him for any extra expenses that might have occurred(Luke 10:25-35).

The spiritual truth to this parable is that a neighbor is anyone you come in close contact with and is in need; regardless of race, color, social or financial status.

Obedience and Service

In these parables, Jesus taught on obedience and the ability to serve. He taught that God gives men gifts according to their abilities. He then holds them accountable for what they do with them. God expects His people to be obedient to His word and use their gifts responsibly. He rewards faithfulness and productivity in His people.

The Loaned Money

In this parable, Jesus told of a man who was going away on a trip. He called his servants to him and entrusted his property to them. He gave each man according to his ability. One man was given five talents of money, another one two talents and the last man received one talent. The first two men put their money to work and doubled it. The man with the one talent hid his. When the master arrived back home, he was pleased with the report of the first two men as to them doubling their talents and said to them, "Well done, good and faithful servants! You have been faithful with a few things; I will put you in charge of many things." The man with the one talent told the master that he was afraid and that he had hidden it. The servant was scolded for his laziness, and was told that he should have put it in the bank to make interest since he did nothing else with it. Jesus said, "Take the talent from him and give it to the one who has the ten talents. For everyone who has will be given more, and he will have an abundance. Whoever does not have, even what he has will be taken from him.

And throw that worthless servant outside, into the darkness, where there will be weeping and gnashing of teeth," (Matthew 25:14-30).

The spiritual truth in this parable is twofold. The first one is that God expects the believer to be obedient, and the second one is that God expects them to be productive and serve diligently.

Prayer

In this parable, Jesus taught that man should always pray, and learn how to wait on the Lord with the expectations that He will answer his prayers.

The Persistent Widow

Jesus told the parable of a widow who kept going before an ungodly judge asking him for justice against her adversary. She went before him time and time again. Each time he refused her, she went back again asking for the same thing. Finally, he granted her the justice she was seeking because she kept on bothering him about it. Jesus said, "And the Lord said, 'Listen to what the unjust judge says. And will not God bring about justice for His chosen ones, who cry out to Him day and night? Will he keep putting them off? I tell you, he will see that they get justice, and quickly,'" (Luke 18:1-8).

The spiritual truth of this parable is that believers must be persistent in what they are praying for, and it is in order to ask again and again until they get their answer.

Repentance

In this parable, Jesus taught that God forgives and gives His people many chances to repent of their wrongdoings and turn to Him. If man chooses not to do so, he will suffer spiritual death.

The Unproductive Fig Tree

In calling people to repentance, Jesus told this parable about a man who had a fig tree planted in his vineyard. He went to look for fruit on it, but found none. So he said to the man who took care of the vineyard, "For three years now, I've been coming to look for fruit on this fig tree and haven't found any. Cut it down! Why should it use up the soil?" The man said to leave it up for one more year, and that he would dig around it and fertilize it. He said if it did not bear fruit next year, then he would cut it down (Luke 13:5-9).

The spiritual truth in this parable is that God expects people to turn from their sinful ways and turn to Him. He gives them more than one chance to repent before He takes action.

Thankfulness

Jesus used this parable to teach that all acts of kindness should be acknowledged in some form.

The Forgiven Debt

In this parable, Jesus spoke of two men who owed different amounts of money to the same moneylender. Neither of them had the money to pay him back, so the man cancelled the debts of both. Jesus asked the question, "Now which of them will love him more?" The reply was, "I suppose the one with the bigger debt cancelled." Jesus said, "You have judged correctly," (Luke 7:41-43).

The spiritual truth taught in this parable is that man should always be thankful for everything, whether the deed is large or small.

Truthfulness

Jesus used this parable to show that God knows man's true intentions.

The Two Sons

Jesus told the parable of a father who asked one of his sons to go to work in the vineyard that day. The son said no, but later changed his mind and went. The second son was asked to go to work in the vineyard that day. He said yes, but did not go. The question was asked, "Which of the two did what his father wanted?" The answer was the first son did what his father wanted. Jesus said to them, "I tell you the truth, the tax collector and the prostitutes are entering the kingdom of God ahead of you," (Matthew 21:28-32).

The spiritual truth taught in this parable is that it is dangerous to pretend to obey. God knows the heart of man, and therefore, knows his true intentions.

Wealth

In this parable, Jesus taught that it is more to life than an accumulation of material things.

The Rich Fool

A man approached Jesus and asked Him to tell his brother to divide an inheritance with him. Jesus said to them, "Watch out! Be on your guard against all kinds of greed; a man's life does not consist in the abundance of his possessions." Then Jesus told the parable about the ground of a rich man that had produced a good crop. But he had no place to store all his grain and goods. Then he told himself that he should tear down his barns and build bigger ones to store his grains and goods. Then he told himself that he had plenty of good things laid up for years, and that he should take life easy; eat, drink and be merry. But God said to him, "You fool! This very night your life will be demanded from you. Then who will get what you have prepared for yourself? This is how it will be with anyone who stores up things for himself but is not rich toward God," (Luke 12:13-21).

The spiritual truth in this parable is that believers must not make having materials things of the world more important than God. It is more important to have God than to have things.

HEALER

Jesus went throughout Galilee, healing every disease and sickness among the people (Matthew 4:23b). His ministry of healing showed His compassion for man and that He was interested in the whole person. His acts of healings verified, along with His preaching and teaching, that he was truly the Son of God. Matthew recorded that news spread that Jesus was healing people, so people brought to Him all who were ill with various diseases; those suffering with severe pain, the demon-possessed, those having seizures and the paralyzed, and He healed them (Matthew 4:24). Matthew and the other Gospel writers wrote of Jesus' healing power and of the faith the people had in Him in order to be healed.

A Sick Woman is Healed

A woman who had been bleeding for twelve years came up behind Jesus and touched the hem of His robe. She said as she spoke to herself, "If I only touch His cloak, I will be healed." When Jesus saw her, He said:

> "Take heart, daughter, your faith has healed you." The woman was healed that very moment (Matthew 9:20-22; Mark 5:25-34; Luke 8:43-48).

Two Blind Men are Healed

As Jesus was moving from one place to the next, two blind men followed Him, asking Him to have mercy on them. Jesus asked them:

> "Do you believe that I am able to do this?" They said, "Yes!" Then Jesus touched their eyes and said, "According to your faith, it will be done to you." And their sight was restored (Matthew 9:27-31).

A Man's Shriveled Hand is Restored

It was on a Sabbath that Jesus went into a synagogue and saw a man with a shriveled hand. He said to the man:

> "Get up and stand in front of everyone, and stretch out your hand!" The man stretched it out and it was completely restored, and looked just like his other hand (Matthew 12:9-13; Mark 3:1-5; Luke 6:6-10).

A Deaf and Mute Man is Healed

At one time, some people brought a man who was deaf and could barely talk to Jesus. They begged Jesus to place His hand on the man. Jesus took the man away from the crowd and put His fingers into the man's ears. Then he spit and touched the man's tongue. He looked up to Heaven and said:

> "Be opened!" At this, the man's ears opened, his tongue was loosened, and he began to speak plainly," (Mark 7:31-35).

HIGH PRIEST

In the Old Testament, the high priests were the mediators between God and the Jewish people. They went before God for the sins of the people. Jesus is our great high priest and He is superior to all priests because He is the Son of God. His priesthood is permanent because it was assigned by God. It is through Him and His Priesthood that man can have a direct relationship with God.

The writer of the Book of Hebrews wrote that Jesus became a priest with an oath (the other priests did not). He said the Lord said to Jesus, "The Lord has sworn and will not change His mind: You are a priest forever," (Hebrews 7:20-21). Other places in his book, he wrote of Jesus being the Great High Priest assigned by God. He said in his writings:

> "Since we have a great high priest who has gone through the heavens, who is Jesus the Son of God, let us hold firmly to the faith we possess. For we do not have a high priest who is unable to sympathize with our weaknesses, but we have one who has been tempted in every way, just as we are, yet was without sin," (Hebrews 4:14-15).

"Because of this oath, Jesus has become the guarantee of a better covenant. Now there have been many of those priests, since death prevented them from continuing in office; but because Jesus lives forever, he has a permanent priesthood. Therefore He is able to save completely those who come to God through Him, because he always lives to intercede for them. Such a high priest meets our needs-One who is holy, blameless, pure, set apart from sinners, exalted above the heavens," (Hebrews 7:22 -26).

The apostle John wrote:

"We have one who speaks to the Father in our defense-Jesus Christ, the Righteous One. He is the atoning sacrifice for our sins," (1 John 2:1-2).

ESTABLISHED THE CHURCH

Jesus established the church when He asked His disciples, "Who do you say that I am?" Simon answered, "You are the Christ, the Son of the Living God." Jesus said:

"Blessed are you, Simon son of Jonah, for this was not revealed to you by man, but by the Father in heaven. And I tell you that you are Peter, and on this rock I will build my church, and the gates of Hades will not overcome it," (Matthew 16:16-18).

The rock on which Jesus would build His church has been identified as Jesus Himself and His work of salvation by dying on the cross for the sins of man. There could be no church without the shedding of Jesus Christ's blood. The church, as the body of Christ, was established on the Day of Pentecost which took place fifty days after Jesus' resurrection from the dead, and His ascension back into heaven.

The word "church" has more than one meaning. The first reference is to the church in general which consists of all believers everywhere who follow Jesus Christ regardless of time and place. They believe in their hearts on the birth, death, resurrection and ascension of the Lord Jesus Christ. Because of their belief in Him, His spirit lives in them, and their bodies become the temple of God (1 Corinthians 3:16). The apostle Paul wrote to inform those that as believers of the Lord Jesus Christ that they are a part of the universal church, when he said:

> "You are no longer foreigners and aliens but are fellow citizens with God's people and members of God's household, built on the foundations of the apostles and prophets, with Christ Jesus Himself as the chief cornerstone (that part that holds the whole thing together)," (Ephesians 2:19).

The second reference to the church is God's spiritual house. The apostle Paul said, "God's household is the church of the living God, the pillar of foundation of the truth," (1Timothy 3:15b). This church is a building where a group of baptized believers meet together for worship, fellowship and praise to God. Jesus is the head of the church, as appointed by God. The apostle Paul said:

> "God placed all things under His feet and appointed Him to be head over everything for the church," (Ephesians 1:22).

David, the psalmist, wrote of his pleasure to enter into the house of the Lord when he said, "I rejoiced with those who said to me, 'Let us go to the house of the Lord'" (Psalm 122:1). Peter portrays the church as a living, spiritual house with Jesus Christ as the foundation and cornerstone and each believer as a stone when he said:

> "As you come to Him, the Living Stone, rejected by men but chosen by God and precious to Him. You also like living stones, are being built into a spiritual house to be a holy priesthood, offering spiritual sacrifices acceptable to God through Jesus Christ," (1 Peter 2:4-5).

Paul also said the Holy Spirit gives every Christian the needed special gifts for the building up of the church when he said:

> "It was He who gave some to be apostles, some to be prophets, some to be evangelists, and some to be pastors and teachers, to prepare God's people for works of service, so that the body of Christ may be built up," (Ephesians 4:11-12).

The Purpose of the Church

Jesus being the head of the church intended for the church to have the gospel of Christ proclaimed throughout the world. The purpose of the church is for believers to come together to worship and praise God collectively. They honor Him with service that extends to other believers. The church is one body with many parts but it is united because of what believers have in common, and that is Jesus Christ. The apostle Paul said:

> "Make every effort to keep the unity of the Spirit through the bond of peace. There is one body and one Spirit just as you were called to one hope when you were called-One Lord, one faith, one baptism; one God and Father of all, who is over all and through all and in all," (Ephesians 4:3-6).

The church has been given the responsibility to make disciples so that they will be equipped to represent Jesus Christ in the world.

Just before ascending back to heaven, He gave what we refer to as the "Great Commission" to His disciples when He said:

> "All authority is heaven and on earth has been given to me. Therefore go and make disciples of all nations, baptizing them in the name of the Father and Son and of the Holy Spirit, and teaching them to obey everything I have commanded you. And surely I am with you always, to the very end of the age," (Matthew 28:18-20).

The Growth of the Church

A group of baptized believers led by Peter and John came together and devoted themselves to the apostles' teachings and to their fellowship. They participated in communion and prayer. The apostles did many wonderful and miraculous signs. All the believers were together and had everything in common. They sold some of their possessions and goods, and gave to the ones who had a need. They met together daily in the temple courts. They ate together in their homes, and praised God and enjoyed each other. The Lord added to their numbers daily, those who were being saved (Acts 2:42-47).

Peter and John were arrested for teaching the people and proclaiming in Jesus the resurrection of the dead, but many who heard the message believed, and the number of men grew to about five thousand(Acts 4:1-4). Peter, who was filled with the Holy Spirit, declared that Jesus of Nazareth, who was crucified and raised from the dead, was the stone the builders rejected, has now become the chief cornerstone, the foundation of the church because "There is no other name under heaven given to men by which we must be saved," (Acts 4:11-12).

The Jewish people worshiped on Saturdays, and so did the early church. They met day after day in the temple courts and from house to house, they never stopped teaching and proclaiming the good news that Jesus is the Christ (Acts 5:42). It was later that they began to worship on Sunday, the first day of the week. This was done in recognition of the resurrection of Jesus Christ from the dead, which occurred the first day of the week (1 Corinthians 16:2).

During Paul's missionary journeys, he pointed to Jesus Christ as being the head of the church. As he set up churches while on these trips, he said this about the church and Jesus' headship:

> "God placed all things under His feet and appointed Him to be head over everything for the church, which is his body, the fullness of Him who fills everything in every way," (Ephesians 1:22-23).

> "It was He who gave some to be apostles, some to be prophets, some to be evangelists, and some to be pastors and teachers, to prepare God's people for works of service, so that the body of Christ may be built up," (Ephesians 4:11-12).

> "Christ loved the church and gave Himself up for her to make her holy, cleansing her by the washing with water through the Word, and to present her to Himself as a radiant church, without stain or wrinkle or any other blemish, but holy and blameless," (Ephesians 5:25-27).

Jesus has been seen as: Son of God, Son of David, Son of Man, Savior, Christ/Messiah, Lord, Preacher, Teacher, Healer, High Priest and Founder of the Church. In each role, He served a specific purpose, whether it was physical or spiritual. He was something to everybody who had a need at that time and in times to come. But in life, His mission was not completed yet. He had to make the ultimate sacrifice.

HIS DEATH

After Adam and Eve sinned in the Garden of Eden, God and man became separated. In order for man to be reconciled with God, Jesus had to make the ultimate sacrifice of death on the cross, as was part of his mission for coming to earth to live among men. After much teaching, preaching and healing during His ministry, the time came for Jesus to tell His disciples about His death. He knew that, as was predicted in Isaiah 53, He would suffer at the hands of the elders, chief priests, and teachers of the law, and that He must be killed, and on the third day be raised to life (Matthew 16:21). But it is only through His death and resurrection that man would be saved and, therefore, be granted the privilege of spending eternal life with God, the Father. Jesus' death was a part of His divine mission on earth. He predicted His death and resurrection to His disciples on several occasions. Mark, the gospel writer recorded that Jesus told His disciples:

> "The Son of Man must suffer many things and be rejected by the elders, chief priests and teachers of the law, and that He must be killed, and after three days rise again," (Mark 8:31).

Toward the end of Jesus' ministry on earth, He was betrayed by Judas, one of His disciples. While praying in the Garden of Gethsemane, He was arrested and taken to trial. Although He was not found guilty of any charges, the Jews insisted that He was guilty of claiming to be the Christ. So they marched Him from one court to another to make Him guilty of a crime He did not commit. Again, He was not found guilty of any charges, let alone charges for which deserved the death penalty (Luke 23:13-23).

Jesus was put on the cross, and hung there for many agonizing hours. When the time came, He gave up His life and fulfilled His God-given mission for which He came to earth. He made the ultimate sacrifice to make salvation possible for all mankind. The apostle Paul said, "Christ loved us and gave Himself up for us as a fragrant offering and sacrifice to God," (Ephesians 5:2). When He died for the sins of the world, God broke sin's power over man. He now has a new life in Christ. He is dead to sin and alive in Christ (Romans 6:2-10). Jesus' death was not an afterthought of God. The Old Testament prophet Isaiah prophesied of Jesus' death hundreds of years before His birth. He wrote:

> "But He was pierced for our transgressions, He was crushed for our iniquities; the punishment that brought us peace was upon Him, and by His wounds we are healed. He was oppressed and afflicted, yet He did not open His mouth; He was led like a lamb to the slaughter, and as a sheep before her shearers is silent, so He did not open His mouth. By oppression and judgment He was taken away. For He was cut off from the land of the living; for the transgression of my people He was stricken. He was assigned a grave with the wicked and with the rich in His death, though He had done no violence, nor was any deceit in His mouth," (Isaiah 53:5, 7-9).

In all four books of the Gospel, the writers wrote of the death of Jesus as predicted by Him. This is Matthew's recording of His first prediction of His own death after Peter said that Jesus was the Messiah. He wrote:

> "From that time on Jesus began to explain to His disciples that He must go to Jerusalem and suffer many things at the hands of the elders, chief priests and teachers of the law, and that He must be killed and on the third day be raised to life,"(Matthew 16:21).

The second prediction of His death was recorded by Mark. He wrote:

> "They left that place and passed through Galilee. Jesus did not want anyone to know where they were because He was teaching His disciples. He said to them, 'The Son of Man is going to be betrayed into the hands of men. They will kill Him, and after three days He will rise,'" (Mark 9:30-32).

Luke's recording of Jesus' third time making the prediction of His death:

> "Jesus took the twelve aside and told them, 'We are going up to Jerusalem, and everything that is written by the prophets about the Son of Man will be fulfilled. He will be handed over to the Gentiles. They will mock Him, insult Him, spit on Him, flog Him and kill Him. On the third day He will rise again,'" (Luke 18:31-33).

Just as He predicted, He died. It was a horrendous death of crucifixion, hanging between two thieves. The Gospel Writers recorded Jesus' death on the Cross. Luke wrote:

> "It was now about the sixth hour, and darkness came over the whole land until the ninth hour, for the sun stopped shining. And the curtain of the temple was torn in two. Jesus called out in a loud voice, 'Father, into your hands I commit my spirit.' When He said this, He breathed His last," (Luke 23:44-46).

John said:

> "Knowing that all was now completed, and so that the Scripture would be fulfilled, Jesus said, 'I am thirsty.' A jar of wine vinegar was there, so they

soaked a sponge in it, put the sponge on a stalk of the hyssop plant and lifted it to Jesus' lips. When He had received the drink, Jesus said, 'It is finished.' With that, He bowed His head and gave up His spirit," (John 19:28-30).

Scriptures teach that Jesus' death on the cross fulfilled His purpose for coming to earth to save humankind from their sins. The apostle Paul wrote of these benefits for those who chose to follow Him. He said:

> "He was delivered over to death for our sins and was raised to life for our justification," (Romans 4:25).

> "God made Him who had no sin to be sin for us, so that in Him we might become the righteousness of God," (2 Corinthians 5:21).

The author of Hebrews wrote:

> "Since the children have flesh and blood, He too shared in their humanity so that by His death He might destroy him who holds the power of death, that is the devil, and free those who all their lives were held in slavery by their fear of death," (Hebrews 2:14-15).

Jesus died, was buried, and then raised from the dead by God on the third day. It was through His death and resurrection that death was conquered. He faithfully served His purpose to defeat all evil on earth. The apostle Paul wrote:

> "For, He must reign until He has put all His enemies under His feet. The last enemy to be destroyed is death," (1 Corinthians 15:25-26).

"But it has now been revealed through the appearing of our Savior, Christ Jesus, who has destroyed death and has brought life and immortality to light through the Gospel," (2 Timothy 1:10).

Jesus completed His God-given mission and gave up His life for the sins of the world. And just as He said would happen, after His death, He was resurrected from the dead.

HIS RESURRECTION

After a little more than three years of teaching, preaching, healing, and persecutions, Jesus was crucified on a cross. His body was placed in a tomb, but He did not stay dead. He was resurrected on the third day just as He said He would. On that day after His death and burial, some women who loved Him went to the tomb to anoint His body. Upon their arrival, they encountered an angel of the Lord who had come down from heaven. Matthew recorded that the angel said to the women:

"Do not be afraid, for I know that you are looking for Jesus, who was crucified. He is not here; He has risen, just as He said, come see the place where He lay," (Matthew 28:1-6).

Jesus knew that God was going to resurrect Him, and He wanted His disciples to be aware of what was going to happen to Him, therefore, He spoke of His resurrection on several occasions. After His transfiguration on the mountain and in the presence of His disciples Peter, James and John, He said:

"Don't tell anyone what you have seen, until the Son of Man has been raised from the dead," (Matthew 17:9b).

The apostle, Mark recorded:

> "He then began to teach them that the Son of Man
> must suffer many things and be rejected by the elders,
> chief priests and teachers of the law, and that He must
> be killed and after three days rise again," (Mark 8:31).

Even after His ascension back to heaven, New Testament writers still spoke of His resurrection because of its importance. On the Day of Pentecost during Peter's message, he said to the crowd:

> "But God raised Him from the dead, freeing Him
> from the agony of death, because it was impossible for
> death to keep its hold on Him," (Acts 2:24).

The apostle Paul said:

> "Christ died and returned to life so that He might be
> the Lord of both the living and the dead," (Romans
> 14:9).

After His resurrection, it was very important that the disciples and others actually see the resurrected Christ, and not just hear about it. If not there would still be some who would doubt that He was resurrected. Luke wrote:

> "After His suffering, He showed Himself to these
> men and gave many convincing proofs that he was
> alive. He appeared to them over a period of forty days
> and spoke of about the kingdom of God," (Acts 1:3).

Jesus appeared to those who loved Him first. His most astounding appearance was made when He appeared in the room where the disciples were waiting and said, "Peace be with you!" Luke recorded that they were startled and frightened, thinking they saw a ghost.

Jesus asked them why were they troubled and had doubts in their minds. It was then that He said:

> "Look at my hands and my feet. It is I, Myself! Touch and see, a ghost does not have flesh and bones as you see I have." And while they still did not believe, He proved it further by eating broiled fish in their presence. (Luke 24: 36-42).

The Gospel writers wrote of other instances of Jesus' resurrected appearances. According to Matthew:

> The women who had gone to the tomb to anoint Jesus' body were afraid, yet filled with joy, ran to tell Jesus' disciples that He had risen. Suddenly they met Jesus. He greeted them. They fell to their knees and clasped His feet and worshiped Him. Then Jesus said to them, "Do not be afraid. Go and tell my brothers to go to Galilee; there they will see me," (Matthew 28:8-11).

Mark recorded:

> Jesus rose early on the first day of the week. He appeared to Mary Magdalene, out of whom He had driven seven demons. She went and told those who had been with Him, and who were mourning and weeping. When they heard that Jesus was alive and that she had seen him, they did not believe (Mark 16:9-11).

> As they were eating, Jesus appeared to the eleven disciples. He rebuked them for their lack of faith and their stubborn refusal to believe those who had seen Him after he had risen (Mark 16:14).

Many people had doubts about Jesus' resurrection. For that reason, the apostle Paul argued that if He died and was not resurrected, then their preaching is useless and man's faith is futile; he is still in his sins; and those who died in Christ are lost. He finalized his point by saying, "But Christ has indeed been raised from the dead," (1 Corinthians 15:14, 17-18, 20a).

HIS ASCENSION BACK TO HEAVEN

Jesus' ascension back to heaven was the return of the Son to the Father. His resurrected body was taken up into the clouds. The ascension of Jesus Christ back to heaven was the beginning of His intercessions on behalf of His people here on earth. Scriptures teach that Jesus is now seated at the right hand of God and is interceding for His people. This is where He will remain until His Second Coming. After Jesus made appearances to some of His followers, He appeared to His eleven disciples and gave them the Great Commission. He said to them:

> "Go into all the world and preach the good news to all creation. Whoever believes and is baptized will be saved, but whoever does not believe will be condemned," (Mark 16:14-16).

Mark recorded:

> "After the Lord Jesus had spoken to them, He was taken up into heaven and He sat at the right hand of God," (Mark 16:19).

According to the Book of Luke, before ascending back to heaven, Jesus told His disciples not to leave Jerusalem, but to wait for the gift of the Holy Spirit, for John had baptized with water, but in a few days they will be baptized with the Holy Spirit. After speaking with them, He was taken up before their very eyes, and a cloud hid Him from their sight. As they were looking up into the sky as Jesus was going up, suddenly two men dressed in white stood beside them. They said:

> "Men of Galilee, why do you stand here looking into the sky? This same Jesus, who has been taken from you into heaven, will come back in the same way you have seen Him go to heaven," (Acts 1:3-5, 8-11).

The apostle Paul wrote:

> "Christ Jesus was raised to life and is at the right hand of God, and is interceding for us," (Romans 8:34).

When Jesus ascended back to heaven, He was no longer physically with the believers; but He did as he said He would, when He told His disciples that he would never leave or forsake them. He sent His presence back to dwell in the believer in the form of the Holy Spirit.

CHAPTER FOUR

Salvation

"Salvation is freedom from sin and death," (Nelson's Illustrated Bible Dictionary). It is a gift from God to man because he loves him. It cannot be earned or purchased. God's Word reveals that man is born in sin and, therefore, is a sinner. There is a penalty for sin, but because of God's love for humankind, there is hope for the sinner. It is the gift of salvation. God provided salvation for humankind because man could not save himself, so God sent him a Savior. All man needs to do is believe that Jesus Christ died on the cross for the sins of the world and was resurrected on the third day. The apostle Paul wrote:

> "If you confess with your mouth, 'Jesus is Lord,' and
> believe in your heart that God raised Him from the
> dead, you will be saved. For it is with your heart that
> you believe, and are justified, and it is with your mouth
> that you confess and are saved," (Romans 10:9-10).

The apostle Paul also wrote that all men were dead in their transgressions and sins, in which they used to live when they followed the ways of this world and its ruler Satan. All people are not morally bad, but even they cannot save themselves. Because of God's great love for man, He made man alive with Christ even when he was dead in his transgressions. It is by the grace of God that he is saved (Ephesians 2:3-4). This could not happen until Jesus Christ died, was resurrected and ascended back to heaven. The apostle Paul wrote:

"He chose us in Him before the creation of the world to be holy and blameless in His sight. In love, He predestined us to be adopted as His sons through Jesus Christ, in accordance with His pleasure and will," (Ephesians 1:4-5).

It was through God's divine will and plans, and His love for humankind that Jesus Christ, who being the very nature of God, made himself nothing; took on the nature of a servant, being made in human likeness, took on the appearance of a man, humbled himself and became obedient to death on the cross for the sins of the world (Philippians 2: 6-8). Once a person accepts Jesus Christ as his Savior through faith, the Holy Spirit enters into him to become Lord of his life. An awakening takes place in his spirit and he is now a believer by faith. He then develops an intimate relationship with God. For the rest of his life, the Holy Spirit works in him to bring his moral standards up to God's standards.

GOD'S GRACE

"Grace is favor or kindness shown without regard to the worth or merit of the one who receives it and in spite of what that same person deserves. It is one of the key attributes of God," (Nelson's Illustrated Bible Dictionary). God's grace is voluntary, and is His loving favor given to those He loves. It is through His grace and mercy that man is saved, although he does not deserve it. Peter addressed a group who believed that in order to be saved, one had to be circumcised. He said:

"We believe it is through the grace of our Lord Jesus that we are saved," (Acts 15:6-11).

The apostle Paul said:

"For all have sinned and fall short of the glory of God, and are justified freely by His grace through the redemption that came by Christ Jesus," (Romans 3:23-24).

Not only is man saved by God's grace, but it is His grace that sustains him. The apostle Paul said:

> "But by the grace of God I am what I am, and His grace to me was not without effect. No, I worked harder than all of them, yet not I, but the grace of God that was with me," (1 Corinthians 15:10).

SAVING FAITH

It takes genuine faith to believe that Jesus Christ died on the cross for the sins of the world. It is difficult for many to believe because there are no living eyewitnesses, and realistically, for some, it just seems impossible. But the Bible declares it and man must believe it! Saving Faith comes into place when man believes and trusts in Jesus Christ as Lord and Savior. Upon his belief, he receives the gift of salvation. The apostle Paul wrote, "For it is by grace you have been saved, through faith—and this not from yourselves; it is the gift of God, not by works, so that no one can boast," (Ephesians 2:8-9). From the moment man accepts Jesus Christ as Lord and Savior, he becomes a part of the Christian family.

Because salvation is a free gift from God, this makes Him the driving force in man's acceptance of Jesus Christ as Lord and Savior. Jesus said, "No one can come to me unless the Father who sent me draws him," (John 6:44). God chose man to be saved. As a result of salvation in Christ, man inherits all the spiritual benefits necessary for living a godly life—forgiveness, insight, the gifts of the Spirit, power to do God's will and the hope to have eternal life. Paul taught that God the Father and Jesus Christ have blessed us in the heavenly realms with every spiritual blessing in Jesus Christ (Ephesians 1:3).

Saving Faith in God begins with the acceptance of the knowledge that Jesus is the Son of God, and that He died on the cross for the sins of the world, as was planned by His Father in heaven. Salvation is a free gift from God and is given to all who believes in Jesus Christ. To believe in Jesus Christ is more than agreeing that Jesus is God. It is putting all of one's faith and trust in Him, knowing that salvation alone is in Him. In Jesus' claim to be the Son of God, He said: "I tell you the truth, whoever hears my word and believes Him who sent Me has eternal life and will not be condemned; he has crossed over from death to life," (John 5:24).

It is God's desire that man have faith in Him and in His Word. God's Word is the only truth that is available to humankind. The Bible teaches that the only means of salvation is faith in Jesus Christ. The apostle Paul wrote:

> "You are all sons of God through faith in Christ, for all of you who were baptized into Christ have clothed yourselves with Christ," (Galatians 3:26).

Because of what God did for humankind through the Holy Spirit, man is able to live a holy and righteous life before Him and the world. All he needs to do is trust and obey God.

RECONCILIATION

Reconciliation is the process in which God and man are brought together again. Due to God's holiness and the sinful nature of humankind, the Bible teaches that God and man were separated. They became separated when Adam and Eve chose to disobey God in the Garden of Eden. Because of God's love for man, He took the initiative to reconcile man to Himself. He allowed His Son, Jesus, to die for the sins of the world. Scriptures make it clear that reconciliation between God and man is an absolute necessity.

The apostle Paul wrote:

> "But God demonstrated His own love for us in this, while we were yet sinners, Christ died for us. Since

we have now been justified by His blood, how much more shall we be saved from God's wrath through Him. For if, when we were God's enemies, we were reconciled to Him through the death of His Son, how much more, having been reconciled, shall we be saved through his life! Not only is this so, but we also rejoice in God through our Lord Jesus Christ, through whom we have now received reconciliation," (Romans 5:8-11).

"If anyone is in Christ, he is a new creation; the old has gone, the new has come! All this is from God, who reconciled us to Himself through Christ and gave us the ministry of reconciliation: that God was reconciling the world to Himself in Christ, not counting men's sins against them. And He has committed to us the message of reconciliation," (2 Corinthians 5:18-19).

JUSTIFICATION

"Justification is the process by which sinful human beings are made acceptable to a holy God. When God justifies, He charges the sin of man to Christ and credits the righteousness of Christ to the believer," (Nelson's Illustrated Bible Dictionary). Justification hinges on the fact that Jesus Christ died on the cross for the sins of the world. It is God's grace that man is justified through his faith in God and Jesus Christ. The apostle Paul said, "He was delivered over to death for our sins and was raised to life for our justification" (Romans 4:25). Paul wrote:

"Therefore, since we have been justified through faith, we have peace with God through our Lord Jesus Christ, through whom we have gained access by faith into this grace in which we now stand. And we rejoice in the hope of the glory of God," (Romans 5:1-2).

"The words, 'it was credited to Him' were written not for Him alone, but also for us, to whom God will credit righteousness - for us who believe in Him who raised Jesus our Lord from the dead. He was delivered over to death for our sins and was raised to life for our justification," (Romans 4:23-25).

PROPITIATION

"Propitiation is the atoning death of Jesus on the cross, through which He paid the penalty demanded by God because of man's sins, thus setting mankind free from sin and death. It expresses the idea that Jesus died on the cross to pay the price for sin, which a holy God demanded of man the sinner," (Nelson's Illustrated Bible Dictionary). Jesus never committed a sin of any kind, yet He took on the sins of the world in order to redeem man from the penalty of sin, which is death. The apostle Paul said:

> "For all have sinned and fall short of the glory of God, being justified freely by His grace through the redemption that is in Christ Jesus, whom God set forth as a propitiation by His blood through faith to demonstrate His righteousness, because in His forbearance God had passed over the sins that were previously committed," (Romans 3:23-25 NKJV).

The apostle John wrote:

> "My little children, these things I write to you, so that you may not sin. And if anyone sins, we have an Advocate with the Father, Jesus Christ the righteous. And He, Himself, is the propitiation for our sin, and not for ours only but also for the whole world," (1 John 2:1-2 NKJV).

REDEMPTION

"Redemption is the deliverance by payment of a price. In the New Testament, it refers to salvation from sin, death and the wrath of God by Christ's sacrifice" (Nelson's Illustrated Bible Dictionary). Salvation is only in Christ Jesus through God. He made man free from sin by redemption, meaning Jesus paid a price with His life that man might have eternal life. The apostle Paul taught that all have sinned and fallen short of the glory of God, and are justified freely by His grace through the redemption that came by Christ Jesus (Romans 3:23-24). Jesus said:

> "For God so loved the world that He gave his only son, that whoever believes in Him shall not perish but have eternal life; For God did not send His Son into the world to condemn the world, but to save the world through him," (John 3:16, 17).

The apostle Paul declared:

> "But God demonstrated His own love for us in this: While we were still sinners, Christ died for us," (Romans 5:8).

> "In Him we have redemption through His blood, and the forgiveness of sins, in accordance with the riches of God's grace," (Ephesians 1:7).

Although Jesus has cleared the way for humankind to have eternal life through His death and resurrection, there are some things that man himself must do; namely repent of his sins, be baptized and develop his Christian faith.

REPENTANCE

Repentance is to have a change of heart. It is turning away from sin, and turning to God. The Bible teaches that God's kindness leads man to repentance (Roman 2:4b). True repentance is shown by actions. It is heartfelt sorrow for a sinful deed, along with the act of turning away and going in the opposite direction of sin. It is also a change of mind or a feeling of regret for past deeds (Matthew 27:3). Repentance is a necessary component for all people who expect to spend eternal life with God. After a tragic accident, Jesus said, to the other people, "But unless you repent, you too will all perish," (Luke 13:4-5).

Repentance is the first step in having a right relationship with God. One has to acknowledge that he has sinned, ask God's forgiveness for the deeds or acts, with the intent to never do it again. It is God's pleasure and the angels rejoice in heaven when man repents of his sins (Luke 15:10). When man truly repents, it is because of God's conviction upon his heart. So repentance is given through God's mercy (Acts 11:18b).

The Lord God, Himself, has always wanted man to repent of his sins and turn back to Him. In the Old Testament, He spoke to His prophets about the people repenting of their sins and returning to Him. There was a blessing in it for them. God appeared to Solomon and said:

> "If my people, who are called by my name, will humble themselves and pray and seek my face and turn from their wicked ways, then will I hear from heaven and will forgive their sin and will heal their land," (2 Chronicles 7:14).

The psalmist David wrote a plea of mercy as he repented of his sins against God. He wrote:

> "Have mercy on me, O God, according to your unfailing love; according to your great compassion,

blot out my transgressions. Wash away all my iniquity and cleanse me from my sin. I know my transgressions, and my sin is always before me. Against you, you only, have I sinned and done what is evil in your sight, so that you are proved right when you speak and justified when you judge. Cleanse me with hyssop, and I will be clean; wash me, and I will be whiter than snow. Let me hear joy and gladness; let the bones you have crushed rejoice. Hide your face from my sins and blot out all my iniquity," (Psalm 51:1-4, 7-9).

God told the prophet Ezekiel:

"If a wicked man turns away from all the sins he has committed and keeps all my decrees and does what is just and right, he will surely live; he will not die. None of the offenses he has committed will be remembered against him. Because of the righteous things he has done, he will live," (Ezekiel 18:21-22).

In the New Testament, Scriptures reveal that God requires His people to repent of their sins and turn to Him. Before Jesus Christ began His ministry, John the Baptist came from the wilderness preaching that the people needed to repent of their sins for forgiveness (Mark 1:4). As Jesus began His ministry, He immediately began to preach on the repentance of sins. Gospel writers recorded that He said:

"The time has come, the Kingdom of God is near. Repent and believe the good news," (Mark 1:15).

"It is not the healthy who need a doctor, but the sick. I have not come to call the righteous, but sinners to repentance," (Luke 5:31-32).

Since it is God's desire that all men repent of their sins and be saved, Jesus told the parable of the one lost sheep out of one hundred that was found, He said:

> "I tell you that in the same way there will be more rejoicing in heaven over one sinner who repents than over ninety-nine righteous persons who do not need to repent," (Luke 15:3-7).

After Jesus' death and resurrection, and before His ascension to heaven, He appeared to His disciples and said:

> "Repentance and forgiveness of sins will be preached in His name to all nations, beginning in Jerusalem," (Luke 24:47).

After Peter healed the crippled beggar, he spoke to the onlookers who were astonished at the healing. He told them the crippled man had been healed by his faith and in the name of Jesus Christ. He took this opportunity to say:

> "Repent then, and turn to God, so that your sins may be wiped out, that times of refreshing may come from the Lord," (Acts 3:19).

Man must repent of his sins in order to have a relationship with God. He puts his faith to work to trust God so that his spiritual maturity can begin to develop. This allows the believer to move from the theological to the practical, where he begins to act on what he believes.

BAPTISM

Soon after receiving his salvation, the new convert will be baptized. Baptism is done in the name of our Lord and Savior Jesus Christ. It is a public display of one's faith in Jesus Christ. Jesus was without sin, yet He desired to be baptized by John the Baptist in the Jordan River before He began His ministry. It was at His baptism, as He came up out of the water, that the Holy Spirit descended like a dove and lit on Him (Matthew 3:16). Christians believe that baptism is an act of faith and obedience. Scriptures teach that Jesus commanded His followers to be baptized. It was after his resurrection and before His ascension back to heaven while still teaching His disciples, and giving them His final instructions, He said:

> "All authority in heaven and on earth has been given to me. Therefore, go and make disciples of all nations, baptizing them in the name of the Father and of the Son and of the Holy Spirit, and teaching them to obey everything I have commanded you," (Matthew 28:18-20).

Not only were Jesus' followers commanded to be baptized, but Jesus set the perfect example for them and Christians of today by being baptized Himself. The Bible teaches that God the Father was pleased with Jesus' baptism. Upon His coming up out of the water, a voice from heaven said: "This is my Son, whom I love; with Him I am well pleased," (Matthew 3:16-17).

From Scriptures, it is clear that baptism must take place in the life of the believer, but it has no saving power. Being baptized is merely an outward show to the world that that person has accepted Jesus Christ as Lord and Savior of his life. The apostle Peter delivered a Spirit-filled message to a crowd after the Holy Spirit had come at Pentecost. After the crowd heard the message and being cut to the heart, "They said to Peter and the other apostles, 'Brothers, what shall we do?'" Peter replied:

> "Repent and be baptized, every one of you, in the name of Jesus Christ for the forgiveness of your sins. And you will receive the gift of the Holy Spirit," (Acts 2:37-38).

The Christian church, in obedience to Jesus' commandment, has made baptism one of the church's ordinances. They believe that baptism should be the same as Jesus' was, that is complete immersion into the water.

CHRISTIAN FAITH

The author of the Book of Hebrews defines faith by saying, "Faith is being sure of what we hope for and certain of what we do not see," (Hebrews 11:1). The apostle Paul wrote: "Faith comes from hearing the message, and the message is heard through the word of Christ," (Romans 10:17). Christian faith begins with the acknowledgment that Jesus is the Son of God, and that He died on the cross to save humankind from their sins. After man has been saved through saving faith, he must then develop Christian faith. This becomes his personal (working) faith in God.

Christian faith in God is an attitude of assurance in God and His Word. In order for the Holy Spirit to become active in the lives of believers, they need a relationship with God. This relationship between God and man comes through faith, which is the foundation for the relationship. Through faith, man can commit his mind and heart to God, because he believes what the Bible says about who God is and what He can do. The writer of Hebrews wrote:

> "Without faith it is impossible to please God, because anyone who comes to Him must believe that He exists and that He rewards those who earnestly seek Him," (Hebrews 11:6).

Man has been justified through faith (Romans 5:1a). True faith in God changes a person's thinking and, ultimately, his conduct. The result of faith in God is obedience to Him. It produces good deeds that do not come naturally. Faith ultimately becomes a part of the Christian's attitude, as it is a part of his thinking and being; therefore, it is active and alive. Spiritual actions are a result of faith in God.

Faith in God is the reason men are able to do things that are out of the ordinary, and are not usually understood by others. Faith in God brings about a strong relationship between God and man; so strong that man realizes all things are possible through Christ Jesus. He truly believes that he can do all things through Christ Jesus who strengthen him (Philippians 4:13).

The eleventh chapter of the Book of Hebrews is often called the "Faith Chapter." In this chapter, it reveals the names of some Old Testament characters who demonstrated faith in God. The author's definition of faith helps man to see faith at work in these Old Testament characters that he spoke of when he was teaching on faith. He wrote, "Now faith is being sure of what we hope for and certain of what we do not see," (Hebrews 11:1). The Book of Hebrews gives a list of certain Old Testament heroes who are examples of how to live by faith.

> "By faith Noah, when warned about things not yet seen, in holy fear built an ark to save his family. By his faith he condemned the world and became heir of the righteousness that comes by faith," (Hebrews 11:7).

> "By faith Abraham when called to go to a place he would later receive as his inheritance, obeyed God and went, even though he did not know where he was going," (Hebrews 11:8).

> "By faith Moses' parents hid him for three months after he was born, because they saw he was no ordinary child, and they were not afraid of the king's edict," (Hebrews 11:23).

> "By faith the walls of Jericho fell, after the people had marched around them for seven days," (Hebrews 11:30).

New Testament Scriptures show that faith in God is a necessary component in the life of the believer. The apostle Paul wrote:

> "For in the Gospel a righteousness from God is revealed, a righteousness that is by faith from first to last, just as it is written: 'The righteous will live by faith,'" (Romans 1:17).

> "You are all sons of God through faith in Christ Jesus, for all of you who were baptized into Christ have clothed yourselves with Christ,"(Galatians 3:26-27).

Personal faith in God is shown by actions. James, the brother of Jesus said faith in a man produces actions. He said faith by itself is dead without actions. He believed that actions verify faith (James 2:17). To prove his point about faith producing actions, he used Abraham as an example when he offered his son Isaac on the altar. He said, "You see that his faith and his actions were working together, and his faith was made complete by what he did," (James 2:20-22).

During Jesus' ministry on earth, he performed many miracles for those who believed. But when He went into His own hometown and began to teach the people, they were amazed at His teachings because He grew up there, and they knew Him and his family. Because they knew His family, they took offense at Him. The Gospel writer said, "He did not do many miracles there because of their lack of faith," (Matthew 13:58).

Faith in God will have some astounding results. The Bible tells of some people who found themselves in what seemed to be some impossible predicaments, but their faith in God made the seemingly impossible, possible. The act of displaying faith in God allows Him to do a good work in humankind. In the New Testament, Jesus speaks of the results of faith. A man had taken his demon-possessed son to the disciples to be healed, but they could not heal him. When the boy was brought to Jesus to be healed, Jesus healed him. The disciples came to Jesus and asked, "Why could we not drive the demon out?" Jesus answered them by saying:

> "Because you have so little faith; I tell you the truth, if you have faith as small as a mustard seed, you can say to this mountain, 'Move from here to there' and it will move. Nothing will be impossible for you," (Matthew 17:14-21).

A woman who had been bleeding for twelve years came up from behind Jesus, and touched the hem of his cloak. Speaking to herself, she said, "If I only touch His cloak, I will be healed." Jesus turned and saw her, and said:

> "Take heart, daughter, your faith has healed you." The woman was healed at that moment," (Matthew 9:20-22).

Two blind men that were following Jesus yelled out, "Have mercy on us, Son of David!" Jesus said to them:

> "Do you believe that I am able to do this?" They both answered, "Yes Lord." He touched their eyes and said, 'According to your faith, it will be done unto you!' Their sight was restored unto them (Matthew 9:27-30a).

A man brought his demon-possessed son to Jesus to be healed. He said, "If you can do anything, take pity on us and help us." Jesus said:

> "Everything is possible for him who believes." The father said, "I do believe; help me overcome my unbelief." Jesus rebuked the evil spirit, and the boy was healed (Mark 9:22b-26).

Christian faith causes things to happen that do not and cannot happen in the natural. As in the story of Abraham, The apostle Paul wrote in regards to him that he was fully persuaded that God had power to do what He had promised (Romans 4:21). God promised him, a 100-year-old man and his 90-year-old wife, Sarah, that they would have a child. Under ordinary circumstances this was impossible, but they had faith in God, and as a result, the promised child was born unto them. Jesus taught that all things are possible, if one can just have faith in God. In teaching His disciples about praying, Jesus said to them:

> "Have faith in God; I tell you the truth, if anyone says to this mountain, 'Go, throw yourself in the sea,' and does not doubt in his heart but believe that what he says will happen, it will be done for him," (Mark 11:22-23).

When Jesus' apostles asked Him to increase their faith, He answered:

> "If you have faith as small as a mustard seed, you can say to this mulberry tree, 'Be uprooted and planted in the sea, and it will obey you,'" (Luke 17:5-6).

The apostle Paul wrote:

> "We live by faith, not by sight," (2 Corinthians 5:7).

Although the believer is saved and is a part of the holy family of God, he or she needs the guidance of the Holy Spirit in their lives. Just before Jesus was to die, He assured His disciples that He would still be with them. He promised to send the Counselor who is the Holy Spirit that will live in them and convict the world of guilt in regards to sin and righteousness (John 16:7-9).

CHAPTER FIVE

The Holy Spirit

"The Holy Spirit is the third person of the Trinity, who exercises the power of the Father and the Son in creation and redemption," (Nelson's Illustrated Bible Dictionary). He is the helper that Jesus promised to send back to His disciples after His ascension back to heaven. He is not visible as Jesus was, but His presence in the Christian is real. "The Holy Spirit appears in the Gospel of John as the power by which Christians are brought to faith and helped to understand their walk with God. He brings a person to new birth," (Nelson's Illustrated Bible Dictionary).

Jesus knew that His disciples needed someone to lead and guide them after He was no longer with them. So He promised them that He would never leave them alone. He promised to send them some help. He said to His disciples, "If you love me, you will obey what I command. And I will ask the Father, and He will give you another Counselor to be with you forever," (John 14:15-16). Although Jesus is no longer here in His physical body, He is here spiritually through the Holy Spirit who is invisible, but yet alive.

THE TRINITY

The Holy Spirit is the third person of the Trinity; that is, He coexists along with God, the Father and His Son, Jesus Christ. Through Him, God and Jesus Christ are spiritually present in the believer. "The doctrine of the trinity means that within the being and activity of the one God, there are three distinct persons: Father, Son and Holy Spirit," (Nelson's Illustrated Bible Dictionary). The word "Trinity" does not appear in the Bible at all, but Scriptures refer to this concept. Some theologians believe and teach that the Holy Spirit and Jesus were present during the creation of the world. The Bible says that when it was time for God to create man, He spoke to someone, saying, "Let us make man in our image, in our likeness," (Genesis 1:26a).

When in one passage, the names of God, the Father, Jesus, the Son and the Holy Spirit are referenced, then it is referred to as the "Trinity." God, the Father, Jesus Christ, the Son of God, and the Holy Spirit all had and have a role in the salvation of mankind. God the Father is the Creator, Jesus is the Savior and the Holy Spirit is the Sustainer. In the New Testament, the Gospel writers, as well as Paul, referred to the Trinity. Matthew referred to the Trinity when he wrote about what he saw and heard at Jesus' baptism by John the Baptist. He said:

> "As soon as Jesus was baptized, He went up out of the water. At that moment heaven was opened, and He saw the Spirit of God descending like a dove; and lighting on Him. And a voice from heaven said, 'This is my Son, whom I love; with Him I am well pleased,'" (Matthew 3:16-17).

Jesus referred to the Trinity as He gave His final commands to His disciples:

> "Therefore go and make disciples of all nations, baptizing them in the name of the Father and of the Son and of the Holy Ghost," (Matthew 28:19).

The apostle Paul recorded:

> "May the grace of the Lord Jesus Christ, and the love of God, and the fellowship of the Holy Spirit be with you all," (2 Corinthians 13:14).

The apostle John wrote:

> "For there are three that bear witness in heaven; the Father, the Word and the Holy Spirit; and these three are one," (1 John 5:7 NKJV).

THE PROMISE OF THE HOLY SPIRIT

During Jesus' ministry on earth, and before His death on the cross, He promised His disciples that He would send the Holy Spirit to live in the believer. At that time, the Holy Spirit had not yet been sent because Jesus had not yet been glorified (John 7: 39b). In regards to the promised Holy Spirit to be sent by God, Jesus referred to Him as the Counselor because He was going to lead and guide God's people in God's way. He said:

> "But the Counselor, the Holy Spirit, whom the Father will send in my name, will teach you all things and will remind you of everything I have said to you," (John 14:26).

> "When the Counselor comes, whom I will send to you from the Father, the Spirit of truth who goes out from the Father, He will testify about me," (John 15:26).

Toward the end of His life on earth, He said to His disciples:

> "Now I am going to Him who sent me. But I tell you the truth: It is for your good that I am going away. Unless I go away, the Counselor will not come to you; but if I go, I will send Him to you," (John 16:5a, 7).

THE SPIRIT OF GOD IN OLD TESTAMENT DAYS

The Holy Spirit has always had His place and function in the life of people. In the Old Testament days, when God had an important job to be done, He chose a person to do it, and the Holy Spirit equipped that person by giving him the needed power and ability to get the job done. Old Testament Scriptures tell of instances where the Spirit of God came upon individuals for the sole purpose of the designated ones to be able to complete certain tasks assigned to them to do by God. Moses went before God with a complaint of the Israelite that they had no meat to eat. God told him to bring Him seventy of Israel's elders who are known as leaders and officials among the people. Moses recorded:

> "The Lord came down in the cloud and spoke with Moses, and He took of the Spirit that was on him and put the Spirit on the seventy elders. When the Spirit rested on them, they prophesied but they did not do so again" (Numbers 11:10-25).

Samson, according to the angel of the Lord who visited his mother, was born to be a Nazirite set apart to God from birth. Scripture says:

> "The boy grew and the Lord blessed him, and the Spirit of the Lord began to stir him." As a young man, Samson and his parents were on a trip when suddenly a young lion came roaring toward him. "The Spirit of the Lord came upon him in power so that he tore the lion apart with his bare hands," (Judges 14:1-6).

David, a shepherd boy, was chosen by God to be king of Israel. God told Samuel to anoint him with oil. The Bible says:

> "From that day on the Spirit of the Lord came upon David in power," (1Samuel 16:13).

THE HOLY SPIRIT IN THE LIFE OF JESUS CHRIST

The Holy Spirit was present, and played a very important role before and after the birth of Jesus Christ. He was active in Jesus' life from His conception to His death. Concerning His birth, Matthew wrote:

> "His mother Mary was pledged to be married to Joseph, but before they came together, she was found to be with child through the Holy Spirit," (Matthew 1:18).

After His Baptism Matthew said:

> "Then Jesus was led by the Spirit into the desert to be tempted by the devil," (Matthew 4:1).

After Jesus' death, resurrection, and before His ascension, He met with His disciples in Jerusalem. He told them:

> "Do not leave Jerusalem, but wait for the gift my Father promised, which you have heard me speak about. For John baptized with water, but in a few days you will be baptized with the Holy Spirit," (Acts 1:4b-5).

After Jesus' ascension back to heaven, He sent the Holy Spirit to live in all believers as He promised He would. On that Day of Pentecost, John the Baptist's prophecy was fulfilled when he said:

> "I baptize you with water for repentance. But after me will come one who is more powerful than I, whose sandals I am not fit to carry. He will baptize you with the Holy Spirit and with fire," (Matthew 3:11).

THE APPEARANCE OF THE HOLY SPIRIT

It was forty days after Jesus' resurrection and ten more days after His ascension back to heaven that He sent the Holy Spirit back to earth to comfort, lead and guide his people, just as He said He would

(Acts 2:2-4). The Holy Spirit appeared on the Day of Pentecost to fulfill His divine purpose, which is to help believers in their Christian walk. The Gospel writer Luke recorded this account of the appearance of the Holy Spirit:

> "When the Day of Pentecost came, they were all together in one place. There were three evidences of the Holy Spirit's presence. The first one was 'a sound like the blowing of a violent wind came from heaven and filled the whole house where they were sitting.' The second piece of evidence was that 'they saw what seemed to be tongues of fire that separated and came to rest on each of them.' And finally, 'All of them were filled with the Holy Spirit and began to speak in other tongues as the Spirit enabled them,'" (Acts 2:1-4).

Being filled with the Holy Spirit meant that they were under the Holy Spirit's control so that His power is seen through their words and actions. The disciples spoke clearly and intelligently in different languages. The people there were from many nations and spoke many languages and, therefore, were amazed that the disciples were speaking in their native tongue (Acts 2:5-12). On this day, the Holy Spirit, whom Jesus told His disciples would come as their Comforter came. He said, "For John baptized with water, but in a few days, you will be baptized with the Holy Spirit," (Acts 1:5).

The prophecy of the prophet Joel was also fulfilled on this day. It was said that the disciples were drunk because of their behavior on the Day of Pentecost. Peter explained that they were not drunk, but that the prophecy of the prophet Joel was being fulfilled. He quoted what Joel said:

> "In the last days, God says, I will pour out my Spirit on all people. Your sons and daughters will prophesy; your young men will see visions; your old men will dream dreams. Even on my servants, both men and

women, I will pour out my Spirit in those days, and they will prophesy," (Acts 2:14-18).

According to the prophet Joel, God said, "And afterward, I will pour out my Spirit on all people," (Joel 2:28a). God provided His people with the Holy Spirit so that after Jesus was no longer with them on earth, God would be spiritually present with and within them through the Holy Spirit. The entrance of the Holy Spirit into the believer's life is the beginning of a personal relationship with God.

THE NATURE OF THE HOLY SPIRIT

The Holy Spirit is the power that lives within the believer. He leads and guides him in this life that he will ultimately have eternal life with God. Jesus said, "I tell you the truth, no one can enter the kingdom of God unless he is born of water and the Spirit," (John 3:5). The nature of the Holy Spirit is revealed by Jesus as He taught about the coming of the Holy Spirit:

He is as the Presence of Jesus Christ

"Therefore go and make disciples of all nations, baptizing them in the name of the Father and of the Son and of the Holy Spirit, and teaching them to obey everything I have commanded you. And surely I am with you always, to the very end of the age," (Matthew 28:19-20).

He is Living Water

"If anyone is thirsty, let him come to me and drink. Whoever believes in me as the Scripture has said, streams of living water will flow from within him. By this He meant the Spirit, whom those who believed in Him were later to receive," (John 7:37b-39).

He is the Spirit of Truth

> "I will ask the Father and He will give you another Counselor to be with you forever-the Spirit of Truth," (John 14:16-17a).

He is a Teacher

> "But the Counselor, the Holy Spirit, whom the Father will send in my name will teach you all things and will remind you of everything I have said to you," (John 14:26).

He is the Spirit of Wisdom and Revelations

The apostle said:

> "I keep asking God of our Lord Jesus Christ, the glorious Father, may give you the Spirit of wisdom and revelation so that you may know Him better," (Ephesians 1:17).

He is the Spirit of Power, Love and Self-Discipline

> "God did not give us a spirit of fear, but a Spirit of power, of love and of self-discipline,"
> (2 Timothy 1:7).

CHARACTER TRAITS OF THE HOLY SPIRIT

The Holy Spirit, being the third part of the Trinity, has His own character traits. He has His own purpose and function in the life of the Christian. During Jesus' ministry, He made the disciples aware that the Holy Spirit is a Counselor who will lead, guide and play a very important part in the life of His followers. On different occasions, He said:

The Holy Spirit Speaks Through Man

"But when they arrest you, do not worry about what to say or how to say it. At that time you will be given what to say, for it will not be you speaking, but the Spirit of your Father speaking through you," (Matthew 10:19-20).

He Gives Life

"The Spirit gives life, the flesh counts for nothing. The words I have spoken to you are spirit and they are life," (John 6:63).

He is with Humankind Forever

"And I will ask the Father, and He will give you another Counselor to be with you forever," (John 14:16).

He Will Testify of Jesus

"When the Counselor comes, whom I will send to you from the Father, the Spirit of truth who goes out from the Father, He will testify about Me," (John 15:26).

He Will Guide into All Truth

"But when He, the Spirit of truth, comes, He will guide you into all truth. He will not speak on His own; He will speak only what He hears, and He will tell you what is yet to come," (John 16:13).

He Will Bring Glory to Jesus

> "He will bring glory to Me by taking from what is mine and making it known to you. All that belongs to the Father is mine. That is why I said the Spirit will take from what is mine and make it known to you," (John 16:14-15).

In writing to the various churches, the apostle Paul said this about what the Holy Spirit does:

He Tells Man He is Loved by God

> "And hope does not disappoint us, because God has poured out His love into our hearts by the Holy Spirit, whom He has given us," (Romans 5:5).

He Lets Man Know He Belongs to God

> "The Spirit Himself testifies with our spirit that we are God's children. Now if we are children, then we are heirs of God and co-heirs with Christ," (Romans 8:16-17a).

He Makes Intercessions for Believers

> "The Spirit helps us in our weakness. We do not know what we ought to pray for, but the Spirit Himself intercedes for us with groans that words cannot express. And He who searches our hearts know the mind of the Spirit, because the Spirit intercedes for the saints in accordance with God's will," (Romans 8:26-27).

He Reveals Things to the Believer

"It is written, 'No eye has seen, no ear has heard, no mind has conceived what God has prepared for those who love Him,' but God has revealed it to us by His Spirit," (1Corinthians 2:9-10a).

He Searches All Things

"The Spirit searches all things, even the deep things of God. For who among men knows the thoughts of a man except the man's spirit within him. In the same way no one knows the thoughts of God except the Spirit of God," (1Corinthians 2:10b-11).

He Guarantees Man's Inheritance

"And you also were included in Christ when you heard the word of truth, the gospel of your salvation. Having believed you were marked in Him with a seal, the promised Holy Spirit, who is a deposit guaranteeing our inheritance until the redemption of those who are God's possession-to the praise of His glory," (Ephesians 1: 13-14).

According to the apostle Paul, if anyone belongs to Christ, He is filled with the Holy Spirit (Romans 8:9). After he makes Jesus Christ, Lord and Savior of his life, the Spirit of God becomes alive in him. Being filled with the Holy Spirit, the believer is no longer controlled by the sinful nature but by the Spirit of God. He then becomes dead to sin, and alive in Christ. Paul said, "But if Christ is in you, your body is dead because of sin, yet your spirit is alive because of righteousness," (Roman 8:9-10).

CHAPTER SIX

Sanctification

"**S**anctification is the process of God's grace by which the believer is separated from sin and becomes dedicated to God's righteousness," (Nelson's Illustrated Bible Dictionary). It is based on the death of Jesus Christ. Men are sanctified in Christ Jesus by His blood that was shed for our sins, and are therefore called to be holy (1 Corinthians 1:2). He actually makes man holy because he was never meant to be impure, but to live a holy life (1 Thessalonians 4:7).

Sanctification is being called out and set aside to do the work of God. That is, man becomes more like Jesus. The apostle Paul said, "For He chose us in Him before the creation of the world to be holy and blameless in His sight," (Ephesians 1:4a). Man comes to Christ just as he is. His thinking has not changed, nor did his attitude, desires or his will. So then should he continue sinning? The apostle Paul said, "By no means! We died to sin; how can we live in it any longer?" (Romans 6:2).

A change takes place in the life of the believer because the Holy Spirit gives him power to live for God. He is free from the grips of sin. The Holy Spirit works from the inside and the evidence will show up on the outside in their behaviors. The apostle Paul wrote:

> "With regards to your former way of life, to put off your old self, which is being corrupted by its deceitful desires; to be made new in the attitude of your minds;

and to put on the new self, created to be like God in true righteousness and holiness," (Ephesians 4:22-24).

He also told believers that their minds must be renewed when he said:

"Do not conform any longer to the pattern of this world, but be transformed by the renewing of your mind. Then you will be able to test and approve what God's will is; His good, pleasing and perfect will," (Romans 12:2).

Paul gave more clarity to the mindset of the person who has a new life in Christ as he wrote about life through the Holy Spirit. He said:

"Those who live according to the sinful nature have their minds set on what nature desires; but those who live in accordance with the Spirit have their minds set on what the Spirit desires. The mind of the sinful man is death, but the mind controlled by the Spirit is life and peace; the sinful mind is hostile to God. It does not submit to God's law, nor can it do so. Those controlled by the sinful nature cannot please God," (Romans 8:5-8).

REGENERATION

"Regeneration is the spiritual change brought about in a person's life by an act of God. That person's nature is changed, and he is enabled to respond to God in faith," (Nelson's Illustrated Bible Dictionary). The Holy Spirit will renew the minds of believers, and their thoughts and ways will become more like Jesus' thoughts and ways. Jesus told Nicodemus, a Pharisee that he had to be "Born Again," (John 3:7b). Being born again merely means that man must have a spiritual rebirth.

In this spiritual rebirth, man puts on a new self through the Holy Spirit. He starts a new life in Christ with a clean slate. God does not hold him responsible for the sins he committed before accepting Christ as his Lord and Savior. His conduct will then begin to imitate that of Jesus Christ. God inspired the author of Hebrews to tell the people: "I will put laws in their hearts, and I will write them on their minds. Their sins and lawless acts I will remember no more," (Hebrews 10:16b-17). Paul knew that once man was born again, a spiritual change had to come. He wrote:

> "As for you, you were dead in your transgressions and sins, in which you used to live when you followed the ways of this world and of the ruler of the kingdom of the air," (Ephesians 2:1-2b).

After being filled with the Holy Spirit, God's people are not comfortable with sin in their lives. Therefore, they strive to live holy and righteous lives before Him and the world. They become sanctified through believing and obeying the Word of God. Christians live in a world that is filled with nonbelievers and, therefore, come in contact with them daily. Some are family members in the same household, some are old friends, some are in places of employment and, some are even in the church. The apostle John wrote in his first letter to the church:

> "Do not love the world or anything in the world. If anyone loves the world, the love of the Father is not in him. For everything in the world-the cravings of sinful man, the lust of his eyes and the boasting of what he has and does-comes not from the Father, but from the world," (1 John 2:15-16).

A change in thinking and behaviors must take place in the lives of the Christian. Things they used to do, they do not do anymore; places they used to go, they don't go there anymore, unless their presence is to glorify God. The apostle Paul wrote, "If anyone is in Christ, he is a new creation: the old has gone, the new has come," (2Corinthians

5:17). The new life in Christ will honor Him in everything the believer does, everything he says and everywhere he goes. Paul also said:

> "Therefore, I urge you brothers, in view of God's mercy, to offer your bodies as living sacrifices, holy and pleasing to God—this is your spiritual act of worship. Do not conform to this world any longer, but be ye transformed by the renewing of your minds. Then you will be able to test and approve what God's will is—His good, pleasing and perfect will," (Romans 12:1-2).

God has set high standards for His people. Mediocre standards are just not good enough for the Kingdom of God. He desires that man live holy and righteous lives before Him and the world. He made this possible through the Holy Spirit. In regards to living as children of God, the apostle Paul wrote:

> "For you were once in darkness, but now you are light in the Lord. Live as children of light (for the fruit of the light consists in all goodness, righteousness and truth) and find out what pleases the Lord," (Ephesians 5:8-10).

The apostle Paul firmly believed that a change in a believer's life was a necessity. He said in his letters:

> "You were taught, with regard to your former way of life, to put off your old self, which is being corrupted by its deceitful desires; to be made new in the attitude of your minds; and to put on the new self, created to be like God in true righteousness and holiness," (Ephesians 4:22-24).

Man must live his life according to the only true doctrines and principles of God. Paul admonishes man to "Continue to work out your salvation with fear and trembling, for it is God who works in you to will and act according to His good purpose" (Philippians 2:12b-13). Paul was persistent that believers filled with God's Spirit of holiness must cross over from darkness into light. And this shows up in their behavior. He declared in his writings:

> "Each of you must put off falsehood and speak truthfully to his neighbor. In your anger, do not sin. Do not let the sun go down while you are still angry, and do not give the devil a foothold. He who has been stealing must steal no longer, but must work, doing something useful with his own hands that he may have something to share with those in need. Do not let unwholesome talk come out of your mouth, but only what is helpful for building others up according to their needs, that it may benefit those who listen. Do not grieve the Holy Spirit of God. Get rid of all bitterness, rage and anger, brawling and slander, along with every form of malice," (Ephesians 4:25-31).

> "Put to death, therefore, whatever belongs to your earthly nature: sexual immorality, impurity, lust, evil desires and greed, which is idolatry. You used to walk in these ways, in the life you once lived. But now you must rid yourselves of all such things as these: anger, rage, malice, slander and filthy language from your lips. Do not lie to each other, since you have taken off your old self with its practices," (Colossians 3:5, 7-9).

> "Do not be yoked together with unbelievers. For what do righteousness and wickedness have in common?" He further said, "Come out from them and be separate," (2Corinthians 6:14, 17).

Although man is born with a sinful nature, God has equipped him through the Holy Spirit to become the spiritual being that He has called him to be. Filled with the Holy Spirit, he takes on a new nature. He becomes holy.

HOLINESS

"Holiness is one of the essential elements of God's nature required of His people. Holiness may also be rendered 'sanctification' or 'godliness.' The word holy denotes that which is 'sanctified' or 'set apart' for divine service," (Nelson's Illustrated Bible Dictionary). God requires that His people be holy because He is holy (1 Peter 1:15-16). Therefore, He sets the standards for them to live by. He gave Scriptures that clearly state that He requires holiness in His people. The apostle Paul wrote:

> "I urge you brothers, in view of God's mercy, to offer your bodies as living sacrifices, holy and pleasing to God-this is your spiritual act of worship," (Romans 12:1).

> "He chose us in Him before the creation of the world to be holy and blameless in His sight,"
> (Ephesians 1:4).

The author of Hebrews said:

> "Make every effort to live in peace with all men and to be holy; without holiness no one will see the Lord," (Hebrews 12:14).

The apostle Peter wrote in his first letter:

> "But you are a chosen people, a royal priesthood, a holy nation, a people belonging to God, that you may

be declared the praises of Him who called you out of darkness into His wonderful light," (1 Peter 2:9).

NEW CREATION IN CHRIST

The Christian is a new creature in Christ. The old man has gone, and being filled with the Spirit of God, the new man has come (2 Corinthians 5:17). His past sins have been forgiven by God, and he begins a new life with Jesus Christ as his Savior. New Testament Scriptures teach that there are benefits for being filled with God's Spirit. Paul wrote that the believer is:

Free and Declared Not Guilty for Sins

"For all have sinned and fallen short of the glory of God, and are justified freely by His grace through the redemption that came by Christ Jesus," (Romans 3:23-24).

Sanctified and Made Acceptable in Jesus Christ

"To those sanctified in Christ Jesus and called to be holy, together with all those everywhere who call on the name of our Lord Jesus Christ-their Lord and ours," (1 Corinthians 1:2).

Forgiven, and Sins are Taken Away

"In Him we have redemption through His blood, the forgiveness of sins," (Ephesians 1:5).

Brought Nearer to God

"But now in Christ Jesus you, who once were far away, have been brought near through the blood of Christ," (Ephesians 2:13).

Adopted into God's Family as His Child

> "He predestined us to be adopted as His sons through Jesus Christ, in accordance with his pleasure and will," (Ephesians 1:5).

Able to Come with Freedom and Confidence into God's Presence

> "In Him, and through faith in Him we may approach God with freedom and confidence,"
> (Ephesians 3:12).

Now that man is dead to sin and alive in Christ, he develops a new outlook on life. Although he has acquired a new nature through Jesus Christ and the Holy Spirit, maturity in Christ is not instantaneous nor is it automatic. It comes by desire, commitment, and a will to be like Christ Jesus. He has to be as the apostle Peter wrote to the Christians in his first letter:

> "Like newborn babies, crave pure spiritual milk, so that by it you may grow up in your salvation, now that you have tasted that the Lord is good," (1 Peter 2:2-3).

Being sanctified, that is set aside by God, man now sees things from a spiritual eye, rather than from the natural eye. The new life in Christ is accompanied by a new nature. He is no longer in bondage to sin. The apostle Paul wrote:

> "For we know that our old self was crucified with Christ so the body of sin might be done away with, that we should no longer be slaves to sin because anyone who has died has been freed from sin," (Romans 6:6, 7).

When man accepts Jesus Christ as his Lord and Savior, he is filled with God's spirit and therefore, should portray godlike characteristics. Although saved and sanctified, he still lives in a world of sin that is influenced by Satan. Yet, he is called to live holy. To live holy and righteous lives before God, Christians must be obedient to God's Word. Peter wrote to the churches that God's people are to be holy because God is holy (1 Peter 1:15). To be holy means to be completely dedicated to God, and set apart for His use. The apostle Paul said:

> "Since you have been raised with Christ, set your hearts on things above, where Christ is seated at the right hand of God. Set our minds on things above, not on earthly things," (Colossians 3:1-2).

Man cannot become holy on his own. In order for him to live holy, he needs help. He needs the help of the Holy Spirit, who will give him the power to live a holy and righteous life. But man must take some initiative to help himself. He must be proactive, and engage himself in activities that will feed the Spirit man. He must spend quality time with God, which will enable him to be strong in the Lord. The apostle Peter said:

> "You are a chosen people, a royal priesthood, a holy nation, a people belonging to God, that you may declare the praises of Him who called you out of darkness into His marvelous light," (1 Peter 2:9).

The new convert should get involved immediately after salvation in various activities in order to learn God's truths. Being active will enable him to grow in his faith, gain wisdom, knowledge, and the understanding of God's Word. The apostle Paul said, "Have nothing to do with godless myths and old wives' tales; rather, trains yourself to be godly," (1Timothy 4:7). Christians should:

Be regular attendees in a Bible-based church for worship services

Develop an avid prayer life (individual and collectively)

Attend Bible Study and church school

Be participants in small group and personal Bible Study sessions

In these kinds of settings, Christians gather together to share their faith and encourage one another in the Lord. To neglect these kinds of meetings can be detrimental to the spiritual growth of a Christian. His spiritual growth will not develop. The author of the book of Hebrews wrote, "Let us not give up meeting together, as some are in the habit of doing, but let us encourage one another," (Hebrews 10:25).

As God's people, who are filled with the Holy Spirit, we are called to live our lives according to the Spirit, in spite of the two conflicting forces living inside us; the Holy Spirit and the sinful nature. The apostle Paul wrote:

> "Live by the Spirit, and you will not gratify the desires of the sinful nature. For the sinful nature desires what is contrary to the Spirit, and the Spirit who is contrary to the sinful nature. They are in conflict with each other, so that you do not do what you want," (Galatians 5:16-17).

The sinful nature consists of all kinds of evil desires mentioned by the apostle Paul, such as, but not limited to: sexual immorality, impurity, corruption, idolatry, witchcraft, hatred, discord, jealousy, fits of rage, selfish ambition, dissensions, envy, drunkenness, orgies. Although the sinful nature is still present in the Christian, the Holy

Spirit controls his life and therefore, overpowers the sinful nature. The apostle Peter wrote:

> "His divine power has given us everything we need for life and godliness through our knowledge of Him, who called us by His own glory and goodness. Through these He has given man His very great and precious promise, so that through them you may participate in the divine nature and escape corruption in the world caused by evil desires," (2 Peter 1:3-5).

As a result of being filled with the Holy Spirit, the believer can live a righteous and holy life as a child of God. Paul gave a list of spiritual qualities that are produced by the Holy Spirit and are evident in the life of the believer. He refers to this list as the "Fruit of the Spirit."

THE FRUIT OF THE SPIRIT

This "Fruit of the Spirit" is the Christian character of the believer. They are attitudes that all believers will have if they allow the Holy Spirit to lead and guide them throughout their daily lives. These character traits will enhance man's ability to live holy and righteous lives before God and the world. When the Holy Spirit is in control, all things are possible. These traits are not something that the believer plans to do, but rather, they are traits that he possesses that guides his attitude and actions toward others spiritually. The Fruit of the Spirit consists of love, joy, peace, patience, kindness, goodness, faithfulness, gentleness and self-control (Galatians 5:22-23).

Love

Love is the first fruit of the Spirit, and everything else is based on it. It begins with God and it compels man to act. God's love is unconditional. It is the greatest of all human qualities because God is love. The Bible speaks of two kinds of love; phileo and agape. Phileo means to have passionate affection and feelings for someone. Agape means to value highly or have high regards for someone.

Love is the key to Christian living. Jesus is talking about agape love when He tells us to love one another as we love ourselves. This kind of love meets the needs of others, without expecting anything in return. There are no limitations on it, and it comes from the heart. Agape love is the very nature of God. It is the kind of love God commands His people to have for one another in spite of their faults.

Agape love is not what a person says, but it is what he does. He is able to be compassionate and merciful to anyone who is in need, regardless of origin, race, social or financial status, or whether he even likes the other person. Jesus showed this kind of love to humankind when He sent His Son, Jesus, to earth to die for the sins of the world (John 3:16). The apostle John wrote in his first letter to believers everywhere:

> "Whoever does not love does not know God, because God is love. This is how God showed His love among us: He sent His one and only Son to the world that we might live through Him. This is love; not that we loved God, but that He loved us and sent His Son as an atoning sacrifice for our sin," (1 John 4:8-10).

Because God is love, it is only natural that Christians will love also, because they are of Him. Man must love God first in order to love his fellowman. This love is expressed in his whole self. His words, thoughts and deeds are all in devotion to God. The whole body of man is engaged when he shows love to God, which forms the love for his fellowman. He cannot love God if he does not love his fellowman, and he cannot love his fellowman if he does not love God. The believer has been commanded by God to love Him and his neighbors. Luke recorded that Jesus said, "Love the Lord your God with all your heart and with all your soul and with all your strength and with your mind, and love your neighbor as yourself" (Luke 10:25-27). God has always wanted His people to love Him and one another.

Old and New Testament Scriptures reveal this to be true. Moses told the people that God said:

> "Do not seek revenge or bear a grudge against one of your people, but love your neighbor as yourself," (Leviticus 19:18).

> "Love the Lord your God with all your heart and with all your soul and with all your strength," (Deuteronomy 6:5).

Jesus said:

> "Love the Lord your God with all your heart and with all your soul and with all your mind. The second is like it: Love your neighbor as yourself," (Matthew 22:35-39).

> "Love your enemies, do good to those who hate you, bless those who curse you, pray for those who mistreat you. If someone strikes you on the cheek, turn to him the other one also. If someone takes your cloak, do not stop him from taking your tunic. Give to everyone who asks you, and if anyone takes what belongs to you, do not demand it back. Do unto others as you would have them do to you. Love your enemies, do good to them and lend to them without expecting to get anything back," (Luke 6:27-31, 35-).

> "A new command I give you: Love one another. As I have loved you, so you must love one another," (John 13:34).

The apostle Paul said:

> "Love must be sincere. Hate what is evil; cling to what is good. Be devoted to one another in brotherly love. Honor one another above yourselves. Never be lacking in zeal, but keep your spiritual fervor, serving the Lord. Be joyful in hope, patient in affliction, and faithful in prayer. Share with God's people who are in need. Practice hospitality. Bless those who persecute you; bless and do not curse. Rejoice with those who rejoice; mourn with those who mourn. Live in harmony with one another. Do not be proud, but be willing to associate with people of low position. Do not repay anyone evil for evil. Be careful to do what is right in the eyes of everybody. If it is possible, as far as it depends on you, live at peace with everyone. Do not take revenge. If your enemy is hungry, feed him; if he is thirsty, give him something to drink," (Romans 12:9-20).

The apostle peter wrote:

> "Love each other deeply, because love covers over a multitude of sins. Offer hospitality to one another without grumbling. Each one should use whatever gift he has received to serve others, faithfully administering God's grace in its various forms," (1 Peter 4:8-10).

The apostle John wrote in his first letter:

> "Dear children, let us not love with words or tongue but with actions and in truth," (1 John 3:18).

"Dear friends, let us love one another, for love comes from God. Everyone who loves has been born of God and knows God. Whoever does not love does not know God, because God is love," (1 John 4:7-8).

"And so we know and rely on the love God has for us. God is love. Whoever lives in love lives in God, and God in him. In this way, love is made complete among us so that we will have confidence on the Day of Judgment, because in this world we are like Him. There is no fear in love. But perfect love drives out fear, because fear has to do with punishment. The one who fears is not made perfect in love. We love because God first loved us. If anyone says, 'I love God,' yet hate his brother is a liar. For anyone who does not love his brother, whom he has seen, cannot love God, whom he has not seen. And He has given us this command: Whoever loves God must also love his brother," (1 John 4:16-21).

Joy

"Joy is a positive attitude or pleasant emotion that is holy and pure. It rises above circumstances and focuses on the nature of God" (Nelson's Illustrated Bible Dictionary). Joy is another one of the Christian character traits that characterizes the believer. The Holy Spirit of God is the source of joy in the believer. God expects His people to rejoice in Him, because joy is of Him. The apostle Paul, who was imprisoned, wrote, "Rejoice in the Lord always. I will say it again: Rejoice," (Philippians 4:4). Even when man is going through trials and tribulations in his life, he is to rejoice in the goodness of God.

Christian will have their fair share of "ups and downs" in life, but they are to learn how to rejoice in all things. David, the psalmist said, "A righteous man may have many troubles, but the Lord delivers him from them all," (Psalm 34:19). The apostle Paul wrote:

"And we rejoice in the hope of the glory of God. Not only so, but we also rejoice in our sufferings, because we know that suffering produces perseverance: perseverance, character; and character, hope," (Romans 5:2-4).

The Bible makes references to joy in God's people. In the Book of Psalms, the psalmists wrote of their joy in who God is, and for all the great things He does, and even for the things hoped for. The psalmist, David wrote:

"Sing to the Lord, you saints of His; praise His holy name. For His anger lasts only a moment, but His favor lasts a lifetime; weeping may remain for a night, but joy comes in the morning," (Psalm 30:4-5 NKJV).

"Restore to me the joy of your salvation and grant me a willing spirit, to sustain me," (Psalm 51:12).

Solomon taught in one of his proverbs:

"There is deceit in the hearts of those who plot evil, but joy for those who promote peace," (Proverbs 12:20).

New Testament Scriptures reveal that Jesus wants His people to be filled with His joy. He said:

"I have told you this so that my joy may be in you and that your joy may be complete," (John 15:11).

"Now is your time of grief, but I will see you again and you will rejoice, and no one will take away your joy," (John 16:22).

The apostle Paul wrote of joy in the life of the believer. He said:

"The kingdom of God is not a matter of eating and drinking, but of righteousness, peace and joy in the holy Spirit," (Romans 14:17).

"May the God of hope fill you with all joy and peace as you trust in Him, so that you may overflow with hope by the power of the Holy Spirit," (Romans 15: 13).

Peace

"Peace is the inner tranquility and poise of the Christian whose trust is in God through Christ. It is a combination of hope, trust, and quiet in the mind and soul, brought about by reconciliation with God" (Nelson's Illustrated Bible Dictionary). This peace has nothing to do with good feelings or the absence of conflicts in one's life. It is of the Holy Spirit who lives in man that lets him know that God is in control of his life, and that he does not have to be anxious about anything. Jesus said to His disciples, "Peace I leave with you; my peace I give you. I do not give as the world gives. Do not let your hearts be troubled and do not be afraid," (John 14:27).

The Holy Spirit enables the believer to experience peace in his life when he is able to trust in God's promises. In both, the Old and New Testaments, Scriptures reveal that God wants His people to have His peace.

God told Moses to tell Aaron and his sons what they needed to say to the people about the peace He gives.

"The Lord turns His face toward you and give you peace," (Numbers 6:26).

Psalmists wrote:

"Turn from evil and do good; seek peace and pursue it," (Psalm 34:14).

"I will listen to what God the Lord will say; He promises peace to His people, His saints-but let them not return to folly," (Psalm 85:8).

In Solomon's words of wisdom, he said:

"There is deceit in the hearts of those who plot evil, but joy for those who promote peace,"
(Proverbs 12:20).

Jesus told His disciples that they can be assured of His peace. He said to them:

"Peace I leave with you; my peace I give you. I do not give to you as the world gives. Do not let your hearts be troubled and do not be afraid," (John 14:27).

"I have told you these things, so that in Me you may have peace. In this world you will have trouble. But take heart! I have overcome the world,"
(John 16:33).

The apostle Paul wrote:

"And the peace of God, which transcends all understanding, will guard your hearts and your minds in Christ Jesus," (Philippians 4:7).

"Let the peace of Christ rule in your hearts, since as members of one body you were called to peace and be thankful," (Colossians 3:15).

When the believer possesses the Spirit of peace in his own soul, He now has the characteristics of a peacemaker. Jesus said to His disciples and other listeners:

"Blessed are the peacemakers, for they will be called sons of God," (Matthew 5:9).

The apostle Paul wrote to the church:

"If it is possible, as far as it depends on you, live at peace with everyone," (Romans 12:18).

Patience

Patience is being able to stand up under suffering and hardships in the midst of adversity. It is the Christian virtue where the Holy Spirit enables the believer to be obedient to God's Word while going through struggles and undesirable experiences, and do so consistently. It is about waiting on and trusting God to act while in the middle of a crisis. The Holy Spirit that lives in the believer gives him the power to endure.

As God is patient with man, so must man be patient with God and his fellowman. He must learn how to wait on the Lord. The apostle Peter mentions perseverance along with other Christian character traits as being acts of faith. He said, "For if you possess these qualities in increasing measure, they will keep you from being ineffective and unproductive in your knowledge of our Lord Jesus Christ," (2 Peter 1:8). Old Testament writers wrote Scriptures that encourage Christians to be patient. David said:

"Wait for the Lord; be strong and take heart and wait for the Lord," (Psalm 27:14).

"Be still before the Lord and wait patiently for Him; do not fret when men succeed in their ways, when they carry out their wicked schemes," (Psalm 37:7).

King Solomon wrote in his great wisdom:

> "A patient man has great understanding, but a quick-tempered man displays folly,"
>
> (Proverbs 14:29).

New Testament writers wrote that patience is an essential trait in the life of the Christian. The apostle Paul believed that there is a reward for those who patiently and persistently do good. He said:

> "To those who by persistence in doing good seek glory, honor and immortality, He will give eternal life," (Romans 2:7).

> "Let us not become weary in doing good for at the proper time we will reap a harvest if we do not give up," (Galatians 6:9).

The author of the Book of Hebrews wrote that there is a reward of God's promises when man can learn to be patient. He said:

> "You need to persevere so that when you have done the will of God, you will receive what he has promised," (Hebrews 10:36).

James, the brother of Jesus, wrote:

> "Count it all joy when you fall into various trials. Knowing that the testing of your faith produces patience; But let patience have its perfect work, that you may be perfect and complete, lacking nothing," (James 1:2-4 NKJV).

Kindness

Kindness (longsuffering) is another Christian character trait produced by the Holy Spirit in the life of the Christian. It is love in action. The apostle Paul said, "Be completely humble and gentle; be patient, bearing with one another in love," (Ephesians 4:2). Kindness is having the ability to consistently show compassion to others, opposed to judging them, when they just can't seem to say it, do it, or just get it right. Just as God is kind to man, so must man be kind to one another. New Testament Scriptures speak of the kindness God expects His people to have for one another. The apostle Paul wrote:

> "Be kind and compassionate to one another, forgiving each other, just as in Christ, God forgave you," (Ephesians 4:32).

> "As God's chosen people, holy and dearly beloved, clothe yourselves with kindness,"
> (Colossians 3:12a).

Goodness

"Goodness is the quality of being good; praiseworthy character; moral excellence," (Nelson's Illustrated Bible Dictionary). Goodness is an essential part of the life of the believer. When the Holy Spirit is in control of his life, He will produce goodness in him. All good deeds done by the believer are done by putting God first in the decision-making. Scriptures speaking to the goodness of God's people are found in both the Old and New Testaments. The psalmist David wrote:

> "Surely goodness and love will follow me all the days of my life, and I will dwell in the house of the Lord forever," (Psalm 23:6).

Jesus said:

> "The good man brings good things out of the good stored up in him," (Matthew 12:35a).

The apostle Paul wrote:

> "Do not be overcome by evil, but overcome evil with good," (Romans 12:21).

> "And we pray this in order that you may live a life worthy of the Lord and may please Him in every way: bearing fruit in every good work, growing in the knowledge of God," (Colossians 1:10).

God is good and because of this, He calls for the believer to show goodness in his dealings with others.

Faithfulness

"Faith is being sure of what we hope for and certain of what we do not see," (Hebrews 11:1). Faithfulness is that godly characteristic in the Christian that shows confidence in God and His Word, knowing that He is who He says He is and will do what He says He will do. In man's most difficult times, he knows that God is always with him. Faith comes from God through the Holy Spirit. "Faithfulness is dependability, loyalty and stability, particularly as it describes God in His relationship to human believers," (Nelson's Illustrated Bible Dictionary).

God is faithful to man, so must man be faithful to Him and others as well in all his dealings. A man is found to be faithful in what he does, and not in what he says. The apostle Paul wrote, "Now it is required that those who have been given trust prove faithful," (1Corinthians 4:2). Displaying faith is putting trust in what God said He would do, whether it is understood or not. Faith does not stand alone, actions must accompany it. When man acts in faith, He is saying to God, "Go ahead. I trust you; have your way, Lord!" Jesus gave a perfect example of faithfulness when He said to His disciples:

> "Have faith in God, I tell you the truth, if anyone says to this mountain, 'Go throw yourself in to the sea,' and does not doubt in his heart but believes that what he says will happen, it will be done for him. Therefore I tell you, whatever you ask for in prayer, believe that you have received it, and it will be yours," (Mark 11:22-24).

Spiritually, the Christian must put forth the effort to be faithful to God and His Word every waking moment. Someone said and I quote, "Using one's faith is like using a muscle: the more you use it, the stronger it becomes." It will make what seems to be impossible in the natural, possible in the spirit world. The believer will see situations as, "Not as he sees it with the natural eye, but what God and His Word has to say about it." During a stressful time in his life, David wrote that God honors those that are faithful. He said:

> "Love the Lord, all His saints! The Lord preserves the faithful, but the proud He pays back in full," (Psalm 31:23).

God inspired New Testament writers to write about having faith in Him. The apostle Paul wrote:

> "We live by faith, and not by sight," (2 Corinthians 5:7).

> "Take up the shield of faith, with which you can extinguish all the flaming arrows of the evil one," (Ephesians 6:16).

The author of Hebrews said:

> "And without faith it is impossible to please God, because anyone who comes to Him must believe that He exists and that He rewards those who earnestly seek Him," (Hebrews 11:6).

The apostle John said:

> "Be faithful even to the point of death, and I will give you the crown of life," (Revelation 2:10b).

Gentleness

Gentleness is another Christian character trait. "It is kindness, considerations, a spirit of fairness and compassion," (Nelson's Illustrated Bible Dictionary). God is kind and gentle with humankind, and expects them to be likewise with each other. The source of gentleness is of the Holy Spirit. It comes with being humble before God and consequently with man. The believer has a spirit of being kind, considerate, compassionate and fair to everyone. The apostle Paul encouraged his readers to possess gentleness as a Christian character when he said:

> "Be completely humble and gentle. Be patient, bearing with one another in love," (Ephesians 4:2).

> "Let your gentleness be evident to all. The Lord is near," (Philippians 4:5).

Self-control

Self-Control is being in control of one's actions or emotions. The source of being able to control oneself is through the Holy Spirit. It is of God and plays a very important part in the life of the Christian.

It allows him to discipline his own body and therefore, is not led by the sinful nature, but by the Holy Spirit.

Self-control is the last one listed of the nine "Fruit of the Spirit" but not considered the least. New Testament writers wrote that self-control is a key ingredient in the life of the Christian. The apostle Paul wrote:

> "You are all sons of the light and sons of the day. We do not belong to the night or to the darkness. So then, let us not be like others, who are asleep, but let us be alert and self-controlled. But since we belong to the day, let us be self-controlled, putting on faith and love as a breastplate, and the hope of salvation as a helmet," (1 Thessalonians 5:6, 8).

> "You must teach what is in accord with sound doctrine. Teach the older men to be temperate, worthy of respect, self-controlled and sound in faith, in love and in endurance. Likewise, teach the older women to be reverent in the way they live, not to be slanderers or addicted to too much wine, but to teach what is good. Then they can train the younger women to love their husbands and children, to be self-controlled and pure, to be busy at home, to be kind and to be subject to their husbands, so that none will malign the word of God. Similarly, encourage the young men to be self-controlled," (Titus 2:1-6).

The apostle Peter wrote:

> "Therefore, prepare your minds for action; be self-controlled; set your hope fully on the grace to be given you when Jesus Christ is revealed," (1Peter 1:13).

Now that man is saved from his sins, he is now empowered by God to live a holy and righteous life, but he still has the capacity to sin. He is not without struggles in his Christian life. Satan will forever be an active force who tries to sway him away from God. There are two forces that are in constant battle within the life of the Christian; the Holy Spirit and the sinful nature that he was born with. The apostle Paul said:

> "For the sinful nature desires what is contrary to the Spirit and the Spirit what is contrary to the sinful nature. They are in conflict with each other, so that you do not do what you want," (Galatians 5:17).

Because of God's love for His people, He gives them the help they need to go up against Satan and his angels. Paul said believers must be strong in the Lord. This comes from trusting in God and His Word. He believed that in their daily warfare, they need to get spiritually dressed for a daily battle with Satan (Ephesians 6:11).

THE WHOLE ARMOR OF GOD

Satan is constantly trying to get back those who have accepted Jesus Christ as their Lord and Savior. The apostle Peter taught that Satan, the enemy, looks for God's people to attack when he said:

> "Your enemy, the devil prowls around like a roaring lion looking for someone to devour. Resist him, standing firm in the faith, because you know that your brothers throughout the world are undergoing the same kind of sufferings," (1Peter 5:8-9).

Satan is a real force, and therefore, cannot be put in the same category as the tooth fairy. He cannot be ignored or overlooked. He and his angels cannot be physically seen, but they are alive and well and appear in different forms and means in people. The apostle Paul wrote:

> "Our struggle is not against flesh and blood, but against the rulers, against the authorities, against the powers of this dark world and against the spiritual forces of evil in the heavenly realms," (Ephesians 6:12).

The Christian has to be led by the Spirit in how to deal with Satan, because he does not have the natural ability to fight off the attacks of the devil. This requires the supernatural power of the Holy Spirit who lives within him. The apostle Paul said, "Live by the Spirit, and you will not gratify the desires of the sinful nature," (Galatians 5:16).

God inspired writers of Scriptures to tell believers how to remain holy in spite of Satan's ongoing attacks. The apostle Paul said, "Be strong in the Lord and in His mighty power." The believer has to get ready for spiritual combat. He needs to be aware that his struggle is basically spiritual and not physical, because the main enemies are evil spiritual beings. Paul taught the church to be prepared for battle when he said, "Therefore, put on the full armor of God so that you can take your stand against the devil's schemes," (Ephesians 6:10-11).

God told Paul to tell the believers to clothes themselves in armor. Scripture says that God did it. The prophet Isaiah wrote, "He put on righteousness as His breastplate, and the helmet of salvation on His head," (Isaiah 59:17a). Since spiritual warfare is done God's way, Paul continues to tell man how to participate in it. In order that he might be able to go up against Satan with authority, he said:

> "Therefore, put on the full armor of God, so that when the day of evil comes, you may be able to stand your ground, and after you have done everything to stand, stand firm," (Ephesians 6:13).

Satan is on his job diligently, and is forever putting forth the effort to attack God's people. So Paul told them how to get suited up to go into battle with Satan, the powerful evil force. Paul painted a visual picture of a list of six pieces of Spiritual armor that is necessary for spiritual warfare. He told them to daily get suited up in "The Belt of Truth, the Breastplate of Righteous, Feet Fitted with the Gospel of Peace, the Shield of Faith, the Helmet of Salvation and the Sword of the Spirit."

The Belt of Truth

When Paul said, "Stand firm with the belt of truth buckled around your waist" (Ephesians 6:14a), he was merely saying the believer should be armed with knowledge of God's word. When he knows the Word of God, then he is able to take a stand on the truth, which is revealed to him through His Word. God's truth does not change, but leads to eternal life. Jesus said, "If you hold on to my teaching, you are really my disciples. Then you will know the truth, and the truth will make you free," (John 8:31b-32).

A man who knows the truth is no longer a slave to sin when he obeys and applies God's Word, as is written in the Bible. He can stand against Satan with God's Word when he is obedient to it, and applies it to his daily living. Reciting the Word of God to Satan in times of trouble helps to resist his attacks as Jesus did when He was being tempted in the desert.

The Breastplate of Righteousness

Next, Paul said to stand firm with the breastplate of righteousness in place (Ephesians 6:14b). He is telling the Christian to live "a godly life" according to God's principles, no matter what is going on in his life seen or unseen. This righteousness comes from God and is by faith (Philippians 3:9b). God is holy and righteous, and therefore, requires that believers live holy and righteous lives before Him. It is in Jesus Christ that man might become the righteousness of God (2 Corinthians 5:21).

The righteous life of a Christian will glorify God because he has a right relationship with both God and man. Satan will do everything in his power to deter the believer from living for God. But the grace of God teaches man to say "No" to ungodliness and worldly passions, and to live self-controlled, upright and godly lives in this present age (Titus 2:11-12).

Feet Covering of the Gospel of Peace

The next piece of protection is for the feet, when he said, "With your feet fitted with the readiness that comes from the gospel of peace," (Ephesians 6:15). He is telling the believer that he should always be ready to go and tell the world that God is love, and that Jesus Christ died on the cross for the sins of the world. All believers are commissioned by Jesus to go and tell lost souls of His love for them. The apostle Paul said:

> "As it is written, 'How beautiful are the feet of those who preach the gospel of peace, who bring good tidings of good things,'" (Romans 10:15b NKJV).

The effectiveness of sharing the message of Jesus Christ depends on knowing the word of God. Man's love for Jesus Christ as his Savior will inspire him to always be willing and prepared to share the message of salvation at all times. His method of presenting the Gospel and his godly lifestyle can encourage others to accept Christ as their Savior. There are unsaved people all over the world and they need to be told the good news, that Jesus Christ died on the cross for the sins of the world.

The Word of God says, "How beautiful are the feet of those who bring good news," (Romans 10:15b). It is Satan's job to try to prevent the believer from spreading God's Word, but the feet of the believer are the only feet God has on earth today to get His message to a dying world. So, the believer must stand on this principle that the "Great Commission" applies personally to him when Jesus said:

> "Go into all the world and preach the good news to all creations. Whoever believes and is baptized will be saved, but whoever does not believe will be condemned," (Luke 16:16).

Shield of Faith

Paul said, "In addition to all this, take up the shield of faith, with which you can extinguish all the flaming arrows of the evil one," (Ephesians 6:16). Faith is the relationship between God and man that allows man to say, "Yes, Lord, I don't see it, but I believe it because You said it." It is trusting God during the most difficult times that everything is going to be alright. The believer's faith is strengthened by believing that God is faithful to His Word. In the Book of Hebrews, the author wrote, "Faith is being sure of what we hope for and certain of what we do not see," (Hebrews 11:1).

Without faith, it is impossible to please God, because anyone who comes to Him must believe that He exists and that he rewards those who earnestly seek Him (Hebrews 11:6). Faith in God puts man in the position to think, believe and say, "I can do all things through Christ who strengths me," (Philippians 4:13 NKJV).

Helmet of Salvation

Next, Paul said to take the helmet of salvation with you, as you get dressed (Ephesians 6:17a). He said the Christian should put on the hope of salvation as a helmet (1 Thessalonians 5:8). The believer knows he is saved and wears the helmet of Salvation faithfully to reject Satan when he speaks negatively about God and His love for him.

The Helmet of Salvation helps man to know that God's Word is right and true. Armed in the helmet of salvation allows man to think on the goodness of God and to ignore the evil thoughts of Satan.

Sword of the Spirit

Finally, Paul said, "Take the sword of the Spirit, which is the Word of God," (Ephesians 6:17b). The Sword of the Spirit, which is the Bible, is the inspired Word of God. God is the author of the Bible, and every word in it can be trusted because God Himself is truth. The apostle Paul said:

> "All Scripture is God breathed and is useful for teaching, rebuking, correcting and training in righteousness, so that the man of God may be thoroughly equipped for every good work," (2 Timothy 3:16-17).

In the Old Testament, God inspired the psalmist David to say, "For the word of the Lord is right and true," (Psalm 33:4a). The Bible teaches man who he is in Christ Jesus and how he should live. It has been said that the Bible is the road map to heaven. The psalmist David wrote about the value of God's Word when he said, "Your word is a lamp to my feet and a light for my path," (Psalm 119:105). Man needs to know God's truths so that his life can be changed by them, for the Word is alive. The author of Hebrews wrote:

> "For the word of God is living and active. Sharper than any double-edged sword, it penetrates even to dividing soul and spirit, joints and marrow; it judges the thoughts and attitudes of the heart," (Hebrews 4:12).

As a believer, it is imperative to know that the Bible is the authorized Word of God, and that he must know it and live it. As a result of the Word living in him, Satan, the enemy of God is not effective with his tricks and temptations. After Paul taught on the necessary spiritual equipment to get man spiritually active in battle against Satan, he said, "And pray in the Spirit on all occasions with all kinds of prayers and requests," (Ephesians 6:18). Paul added that because he knew that prayer is always a necessary component in the life of the Christian.

PHYSICAL / SPIRITUAL TRAITS

There is yet another group of spiritual traits that will enhance man's spiritual growth. They, too, are driven by the Holy Spirit, and are visibly portrayed. James, the brother of Jesus, told Christians everywhere how to come near to God. It is up to the believer to take the initiative in this process. He wrote that man must submit himself to God; he must commit his life to God's will and control, and be willing to follow Him. He must not allow Satan to entice and tempt him in evil doings. He must lead a good clean life, replacing sinful desires with desires to do God's will. Be sorrow for his sins, and humble himself before the Lord (James 4:7-10). These traits are basic and every Christian should diligently take part in them. They are:

Attend Worship Services

Christians attend church to worship God, and fellowship with each other as they have something in common, and that is Jesus Christ as their Lord and Savior. Attending church is important but it does not make a person a Christian. Christians come together to share their faith and to strengthen one another in the Lord. The author of Hebrews said, "Let us not give up meeting together," (Hebrews 10:25a).

Jesus set a perfect example for Christians today. It was His custom to attend worship services during His stay on earth (Luke 4:16). Scriptures support the fact that God expects man to attend worship services. In the Bible, Scriptures refer to corporate worship. The psalmist, David wrote:

> "I rejoiced with those who said to me, 'Let us go into the house of the Lord," (Psalm 122:1).

Another psalmist wrote:

> "I would rather be a doorkeeper in the house of the Lord than dwell in the tents of the wicked," (Psalm 84:10b).

Luke wrote that the apostle Paul said:

> "Be shepherds of the church of God, which He bought with His own blood," (Acts 20:28).

The author of Hebrews wrote that Jesus said:

> "I will declare your name to my brothers; in the presence of the congregation I will sing your praises," (Hebrews 2:12).

Study the Scriptures

When man opens his Bible to study the Scriptures, whether he is in the house of the Lord or at home during his private study time, he allows God to speak to him. When studying the Word of God, man should do so prayerfully. He should ask for wisdom, understanding, and knowledge of God's doctrines and His principles. God's Words are not just mere words, but they are living and therefore are designed for lives to be changed. The author of Hebrews declares that:

> "The word of God is living and active. Sharper than any double-edged sword, it penetrates even to dividing soul and spirit, joints and marrow; it judges the thoughts and attitudes of the heart," (Hebrews 4:12).

Scriptures were given by God to man and compiled in a book called the Bible. This was done so that man can know the way to salvation and also be equipped to do what God has called him to do.

Whatever man needs to know is in the Bible in the form of Scriptures. All Scriptures are inspired by God, therefore are trustworthy. They are written by prophets and apostles, and that makes it authoritative. The apostle Paul said:

> "All Scripture is God-breathed and is useful for teaching, rebuking, correcting and training in righteousness, so that the man of God maybe thoroughly equipped for every good work," (2 Timothy 3:16-17).

Man cannot envision the true meaning of God's Word, but the Holy Spirit living in him helps him to understand the Scriptures. Paul wrote:

> "The man without the Spirit does not accept the things that come from the Spirit of God, for they are foolishness to him, and he cannot understand them, because they are spiritually discerned," (Romans 2:14).

God's people are to know the truth, speak it and live it. This can only happen if he studies, meditates, and applies God's Word to his daily living. The apostle Paul wrote, "Because our Gospel came to you not simply with words, but also with power, with the Holy Spirit and with deep conviction," (1Thessalonians 1:5). In making decisions, the believer needs to know what God says about the matter, after which, he can base his decisions on "What thus says the Lord." In the Bible, God sets the standards for a moral lifestyle for Christians. Everything God requires of His people is in the Bible. It points out sin, but it also tells how to avoid it; and teaches the believer how to live a holy and righteous life with the Holy Spirit as a Helper. It teaches the believer the will of God for his life, so that in the end time, he will spend eternity with Him.

It is very important for the believer to read God's Word, but it is more important that he understands it so that he is able to live it.

Therefore, the believer must study regularly, prayerfully and with a purpose in mind. Paul wrote to Timothy, his protégé: "Be diligent to present yourself approved to God, a worker who does not need to be ashamed, rightly dividing the word of truth," (2 Timothy 2:15 NKJV). In the Old and New Testament, Scriptures were given to let man know that God's Word is valuable in the life of God's people. God said to Joshua:

> "Do not let this Book of the Law depart from your mouth; meditate on it day and night, so that you may be careful to do everything written in it. Then you will be prosperous and successful," (Joshua 1:8).

An anonymous psalmist wrote:

> "The word of the Lord is right and true," (Psalm 33:4a).

David, the psalmist, wrote:

> "The law of the Lord is perfect, reviving the soul. The statues of the Lord are trustworthy, making wise the simple. The precepts of the Lord are right, giving joy to the heart. The commands of the Lord are radiant, giving light to the eyes. The ordinances of the Lord are sure and altogether righteous. They are more precious than gold, than much pure gold; they are sweeter than honey, than honey from the comb," (Psalm 19:7-8, 9b-10).

The prophet Isaiah said to the Israelites, during their captivity:

> "The grass withers and the flowers fall, but the word of our God stands forever," (Isaiah 40:8).

In teaching that God's Word never changes, Jesus said:

> "Heaven and earth will pass away, but my words will never pass away," (Mark 13:31).

The apostle Paul said:

> "Everything that was written in the past was to teach us, so that through endurance and the encouragement of the Scriptures we might have hope," (Romans 15:4).

Live in Obedience to God's Word

"Biblically speaking, obedience is to carry out the word and will of God. It has to do with hearing the word of God and responding to it in a positive manner," (Nelson's Illustrated Bible Dictionary). Humility is the beginning of obedience to God. Man acknowledges the fact that God, his creator and provider, wants the best for him, and that His way is the only way. God wants man to obey His commands, but He does not force him to do so. He gives man the ability to make choices, as he did with Adam and Eve in the Garden of Eden. If man chooses not to obey God as they did, he sins, and sin breaks the fellowship between God and himself. James, Jesus' brother, said:

> "Do not merely listen to the word, and so deceive yourselves. Do what it says. Anyone who listens to the word but does not do what it says is like a man who looks at his face in a mirror and, after looking at himself, goes away and immediately forgets what he looks like," (James 1:22-24).

Obedience to God's Word is more important than satisfying personal desires or doing something to please others. Knowing God's Word is good, but obeying it is what God requires. In the Old Testament, sacrifices by God's people to Him were very important, but He told the prophet Samuel to say to Saul: "Does the Lord delight in burnt offerings and sacrifices as much as in obeying the voice of the Lord? To obey is better than sacrifice," (1 Samuel 15:22a).

Christians should obey God out of love for Him. Jesus said to His disciples, "If you love me, you will obey what I command," (John 14:15). Man must be obedient to God in all things, not just in the areas of his life where it is comfortable or convenient to do so. God expects man to obey the rules of the land, but ultimately, he must obey God's Words over man's manmade rules. Throughout the Bible, Scriptures reveal that God desired His people to be obedient to His Word and rewards them for doing so. Moses said to the Israelites:

> "If you fully obey the Lord your God and carefully follow all His commands, the Lord your God will set you high above all nations on earth. All these blessings will come upon you and accompany you if you obey the Lord your God," (Deuteronomy 28:1-2).

> "I command you today to love the Lord your God and walk in His ways, and to keep His commands, decrees and laws; then you will live and increase, and the Lord your God will bless you in the land you are entering to possess," (Deuteronomy 30:16).

The prophet Isaiah told a rebellious people that these words came from the mouth of the Lord:

> "If you are willing and obedient, you will eat the best from the land," (Isaiah 1:19).

Jesus said as He taught on the importance of obedience:

> "Whoever has my commands and obeys them, he is the one who loves me. He who loves Me will be loved by my Father, and I, too, will love him and show myself to him," (John 14:21).

According to the apostle Paul, punishment is in order for being disobedient. He wrote:

> "He will punish those who do not know God and do not obey the gospel of our Jesus Christ. They will be punished with everlasting destruction and shut out from the presence of the Lord and from the majesty of His power," (2Thessalonians 1:8-9).

The apostle John wrote in his first letter:

> "We know that we have come to know Him if we obey His commands. The man who says, 'I know Him' but does not do what he commands is a liar, and the truth is not in him. But if anyone obeys His word, God's love is truly made complete in him. This is how we know we are in Him," (1John 2:3-5).

God commands His people to obey His Word. Life is in the Word of God, and disobedience to His Word is spiritual death.

Have a Forgiving Spirit

To be able to forgive is to let go of resentment for a wrongness that has been committed toward you. This can be very difficult, but it is commanded by God for His people to do. God is a forgiving God and no sin is too great that it cannot be forgiven, therefore He demands that His people also be forgiving. The apostle Paul said this of Jesus Christ, "In Him we have redemption through His blood, the forgiveness of sins, in accordance with the riches of God's grace," (Ephesians 2:7). God did this for humankind, and surely to require man to forgive his fellowman is not asking too much. Anyone who wants to be forgiven must be able to forgive others who wronged them. Jesus said:

"If you forgive men when they sin against you, your heavenly Father will also forgive you. But if you do not forgive men their sins, your Father will not forgive your sins," (Matthew 6:14-15).

God is the supreme forgiver of sins. He has completely forgiven man for his past sins upon his acceptance of Jesus Christ as his Lord and Savior. Because of God's forgiveness of man's sins, man too, must be forgiving. There is never a limit as to how many times a person should forgive another person for sinning against them. When Peter asked Jesus how many times should he forgive his brother for sinning against him, Jesus said, "I do not say to you, up to seven times, but up to seventy times seven," (Matthew 18:21-22 NKJV). The Bible teaches that it is necessary for people to forgive one another. Jesus taught the importance of forgiving when He said:

"When you stand praying, if you hold anything against anyone, forgive him, so that your Father in heaven may forgive you your sins," (Mark 11:25).

"Forgive, and you will be forgiven," (Luke 6:37b).

The apostle Paul wrote:

"Bear with each other and forgive whatever grievances you may have against one another. Forgive as the Lord forgave you," (Colossians 3:10).

Have an Active Prayer Life

Prayer is a way of life for the Christian. A prayer life is the result of being in a relationship with God. The believer is able to stay in touch with Him about all things and at any time. All prayers should begin with the acknowledgement of who God is, giving Him honor and praise. Prayer time is an opportunity for man to offer thanks and praises to God for His goodness and mercy, and to tell Him about his needs and desires. The most significant part of prayer is not length or posture, but to have faith that God is going to answer all prayers.

Prayer time should be a humbling experience where God increases and man decreases because he knows that God is the supplier of all good things. All prayers must be prayed "In the name of Jesus." As Jesus was teaching about the importance of using His name in prayer, He said, "I tell you the truth, my Father will give you whatever you ask in my name," (John 16:23b). However, prayers of requests must be made with the right motives in mind. James wrote, "When you ask, you do not receive, because you ask with wrong motives," (James 4:3).

Jesus Christ set a perfect example for Christians to follow because He prayed. He prayed to God for Himself, and for the people. When the believer prays, he too, must pray for God's blessing on others as well as himself. James, the brother of Jesus, said, "The prayer of a righteous man is powerful and effective," (James 4:16b). Because God is omniscience, He already knows what man needs or wants. But the mere fact that man is coming to God with his requests pleases God because man is acknowledging that he needs God. Jesus said to His disciples, "If you believe, you will receive whatever you ask in prayer," (Matthew 21:22). When man comes before God to repent of his sins, he must truly be sincere in his asking for forgiveness, and must be remorseful of those sinful acts. God answers all prayers that are prayed in sincerity and are in His will. The Lord said to Solomon:

> "If my people who are called by my name, will humble themselves and pray and seek my face and turn from their wicked ways, then will I hear from heaven and will forgive their sin and will heal their land. Now my eyes will be open and my ears attentive to the prayers offered in this place," (2 Chronicles 7:14-15).

Serious prayer is frequently accompanied by fasting. Giving up food and spending time in prayer is very beneficial to the believer. During fasting and prayer, the believer humbles himself and concentrates on

God and His goodness. There are several types of prayers that God's people pray. They are: Prayers of confessions, Prayers of thanksgiving, Intercessory prayer and prayers of supplication. The apostle Paul said:

"And pray in the Spirit on all occasions with all kinds of prayers and requests. With this in mind, be alert and always keep on praying for all the saints,' (Ephesians 6:18).

Prayers of Confessions

Man goes before a holy God to acknowledge that he has sinned. He must sincerely confess his sins to God in order to restore their relationship.

Prayers of Thanksgiving

Man gives thanks for the blessings God has blessed him with. Things he would not and could not have if God had not provided them for him (salvation, another day of life, good health, shelter, a peace of mind in the midst of confusion, deliverance, jobs, families, friends, government, and much more).

Intercessory Prayers

The righteous man goes before God in behalf of others and their needs.

Prayers of Supplication

Man goes before God to ask Him to supply his needs and the needs of others.

In the Old Testament, God spoke to men telling them there was power in prayer. He said to Job's friends:

"My servant Job will pray for you and I will accept his prayer and not deal with you according to your folly. You have not spoken of me what is right, as my servant Job has," (Job 42:9).

He told the prophet Jeremiah:

"Call to me and I will answer you and tell you great and unsearchable things you do not know," (Jeremiah 33:3).

In Jabez's famous prayer to God in the Old Testament, he made a request, and God answered his prayer. He said:

"Oh, that you would bless me and enlarge my territory! Let your hands be with me, and keep me from harm so that I will be free from pain." And God granted his request (1Chronicles 4:10).

The Bible teaches that Jesus taught His disciples that they should pray and that there is power in prayer. He said:

"Love your enemies and pray for those who persecute you that you may be sons of your Father in heaven," (Matthew 5:44-45a).

"When you pray, go into your room, close the door and pray to your Father, who is unseen. Then your Father who sees what is done in secret, will reward you. And when you pray, do not keep on babbling like pagans, for they think they will be heard because of their many words. Do not be like them, for your Father knows what you need before you ask Him," (Matthew 6:6-8).

"Therefore I tell you, whatever you ask in prayer, believe that you received it, and it will be yours. And when you stand praying, if you hold anything against anyone, forgive him, so that your Father in heaven may forgive you your sins," (Mark 11:24-26).

"So I say to you: Ask and it will be given to you; seek and you will find; knock and the door will be opened to you. For everyone who asks receives; he who seeks finds; and to him who knocks, the door will be opened," (Luke 11:9-10).

One day while praying, one of Jesus' disciples asked Him to teach them how to pray. He said:

"When you pray, say: Father, Hallowed be your name, your kingdom come. Give us each day our daily bread. Forgive us our sins, for we also forgive everyone who sins against us. And lead us not into temptation," (Luke 11:1-4).

New Testament writers taught believers how to pray and what to pray for. The apostle Paul said:

Pray in the Spirit

"Pray in the Spirit on all occasions with all kinds of prayers and requests. With this in mind, be alert and always keep on praying for all the saints," (Ephesians 6:18).

Pray Instead of Worrying

"Don't be anxious about anything, but in everything, by prayer and petition, with thanksgiving, present your requests to God," (Philippians 4:6).

Devote Oneself to Prayer

"Devote yourselves to prayer, being watchful and thankful," (Colossians 4:2).

Have a Prayerful Attitude

"Pray continually," (1Thessalonians 5:17)

Pray for Everyone

"I urge, then, first of all, that requests, prayers, intercession and thanksgiving be made for everyone – for kings all those in authority, that we may live peaceful and quiet lives in all godliness and holiness," (1Timothy 2:1-2).

James, the brother of Jesus, wrote:

Pray for Healing

"Is any one of you in trouble? He should pray. Is anyone happy? Let him sing songs of praise. Is any one of you sick? He should call the elders of the church to pray over him and anoint him with oil in the name of the Lord. And the prayer offered in faith will make the sick person well; the Lord will raise him up. If he has sinned, he will be forgiven. Therefore confess your sins to each other and pray for each other so that you may be healed. The prayer of a righteous man is powerful and effective," (James 5:13-16).

The apostle John wrote in his first letter:

Pray with Confidence

"This is the confidence we have in approaching God: that if we ask anything according to His will, He hears us. And if we know that He hears us, whatever we ask, we know that we have what we asked of Him," (1John 5:14-15).

Pray for Your Brother

"If anyone sees his brother commit a sin that does not lead to death, he should pray and God will give him life," (1 John 5:16).

Have a Humble Spirit

"Humility is a freedom from arrogance that grows out of the recognition that all we have and are comes from God," (Nelson's Illustrated Bible Dictionary). Man must be able to put things in the proper prospective. He has to realize that God created everything including mankind, and because of this, He is above all of His creations. The most supreme example of humility shown to humankind was the humility of Jesus Christ who left heaven to come to earth to die a heinous death on the cross for the salvation of humankind. The apostle Paul said:

"Jesus, being the very nature of God, did not consider equality with God something to be grasped, but made Himself nothing, taking the very nature of a servant being made in human likeness. And being found in appearance as a man, He humbled himself and became obedient to death, even death on a cross," (Philippians 2:6-8).

God requires a spirit of humility in the believer. Man must be able to evaluate himself properly. He should not think too highly of himself because he, too, was created by God as well as others. The apostle Paul said: "Live in harmony with one another. Do not be proud, but be willing to associate with people of low position. Do not be conceited," (Romans 12:16).

God made all men out of the same material, and in the sight of God, no one man is better than another. Granted, some are more physically appealing than others, some are more refined, and still others are more educated and financially stable, but the bottom line is, God made humankind and loves them equally. The gifts and talents that God has blessed people with do not make them any better than anyone else, they are just gifted or talented people. So no matter what man's status is in life, he needs to be able to think rightly about his own place and position in life. Most of all he needs to humble himself before God and man, acknowledging the fact that God is the creator of all things, and therefore is in control of it all. The apostle Paul wrote:

> "Do nothing out of selfish ambition or vain conceit,
> but in humility consider others better than yourselves.
> Each of you should look not only to your own interests,
> but also to the interests of others," (Philippians 2:3-4).

In both the Old and New Testaments, Scriptures tell that God acknowledges humility in His people. The Lord appeared to Solomon when he had finished the temple and said:

> "If my people, who are called by my name, will humble themselves and pray and seek my face and turn from their wicked ways, then will I hear from heaven and will forgive their sin and will heal their land," (2 Chronicles 7:14).

The psalmist David wrote:

> "Good and upright is the Lord; therefore He instructs sinners in His ways. He guides the humble in what is right and teaches them His way," (Psalm 25:8-9).

An anonymous Psalmist wrote:

> "For the Lord takes delight in His people; He crowns the humble with salvation," (Psalm 149:4).

King Solomon said:

> "Humility and the fear of the Lord bring wealth and honor and life," (Proverbs 22:4).

Jesus, as well as the apostle Paul spoke about the importance of humility in the people of God. Jesus said:

> "Everyone who exalts himself will be humbled, and he who humbles himself will be exalted," (Luke 14:11).

The apostle Paul wrote:

> "Remind the people to be subject to rulers and authorities, to be obedient, to be ready to do whatever is good, to slander no one, to be peaceable and considerate, and to show true humility toward all men," (Titus 3:1-2).

James, the brother of Jesus, wrote:

> "God gives us more grace. That is why Scripture says, 'God opposes the proud, but gives grace to the humble," (James 4:6).

The apostle Peter wrote in his first letter:

> "Young men, in the same way, be submissive to those who are older. All of you, clothe yourselves with humility toward one another, because God opposes the proud but gives grace to the humble. Humble yourselves, therefore under God's mighty hand, that He may lift you up in due time," (1 Peter 5:5-6).

Worships God

"Worship is reverent devotion and allegiance pledged to God; the rituals or ceremonies by which this reverence is expressed" (Nelson's Illustrated Bible Dictionary). It is giving Him all the honor, glory and praise, and can be done in various ways. The word "hallelujah" is used to express praise and thanksgiving. Worship to God is done in humility, with man acknowledging the fact that God loves him and is the supplier of his every need. The author of Hebrews wrote, "Let us be thankful, and so worship God acceptably with reverence and awe," (Hebrews 12:28b). Worship is due to God because He is God. The Psalmist wrote:

> "Shout for joy to the Lord, all the earth. Worship the Lord with gladness; come before him with joyful songs. Know that the Lord is God. It is He who made us, and we are His; we are his people, the sheep of His pasture," (Psalm 100:1-3).

The Holy Spirit gets the believer's heart ready for worship, as God is Spirit, and His worshipers must worship Him in Spirit and in Truth (John 4:24). God does not want meaningless worship. He deserves the highest praises because He is God. The prophet Isaiah told the people that the Lord said:

"These people come near to me with their mouth and honor me with their lips. But their hearts are far from me. Their worship of me is made up only of rules taught by men," (Isaiah 29:13).

Old and New Testament Scriptures tell about worship that is due to God. David, the psalmist, wrote:

"Worship the Lord in the splendor of His holiness; tremble before Him, all the earth," (Psalm 96:9).

An anonymous psalmist wrote:

"Come, let us bow down in worship, let us kneel before the Lord our maker; for He is our God and we are the people of His pasture, the flock under his care," (Psalm 95:6-7).

Jesus Himself said:

"Worship the Lord your God and serve Him only," (Matthew 4:10).

"God is spirit, and His worshipers must worship in spirit and in truth," (John 4:24).

Expressions of worship can be in the form of daily prayer, praise in songs, giving of oneself, witnessing, participating in the Lord's Supper, but most of all living a life of holiness.

Daily Prayer

To worship God during daily prayer, whether it be morning, noon or night, is always the appropriate time to recognize Him as Lord God Almighty. This is the time to give thanks for all things, but most of all to thank and praise Him for allowing His Son, Jesus Christ to die on the cross for the sins of the world, which made it possible to spend eternal life with Him. The apostle Paul taught to always give thanks to God, and for everything. He said:

> "Always giving thanks to God the Father for everything, in the name of our Lord Jesus Christ," (Ephesians 5:20).

> "Devote yourselves to prayer, being watchful and thankful," (Colossians 4:2).

A Spirit of Praise

"The praise of man toward God is the means by which he expresses his joy to the Lord," (Nelson's Illustrated Bible Dictionary). It is during praise that the inner man's attitude becomes an outward expression. He is able to forget his problems and everything else that is going on around him, and concentrate on the goodness of God. He expresses his appreciation to God for His love, grace and mercy that He blesses him with daily.

One of the highest commendations the believer can give to God is to praise Him in worship. The psalmist David wrote: "Let the righteous rejoice in the Lord and take refuge in Him; let all the upright in heart praise Him," (Psalm 64:11). God is the only One who is worthy of praise, because He is the Great Creator of all things. God has shown man how much He loves him, now through praise and worship, man expresses his love for God. He realizes that his Creator loves him and withholds no good things from him and therefore, deserves the highest honor and praise. The psalmists praised God because they knew He was worthy of their praise. The psalmist David wrote:

> "Praise the Lord, O my soul; all my inmost being, praise His holy name. Praise the Lord, O my soul, and

forget not all His benefits. Who forgive all your sins and heals all your diseases," (Psalm 103:1-3).

An anonymous psalmist wrote:

"Rejoice in the Lord, you who are righteous, and praise His holy name," (Psalm 97:12).

"Praise the Lord. Praise God in His sanctuary; praise Him in His mighty heavens. Praise Him for His acts of power; praise Him for His surpassing greatness. Praise Him with the sound of the trumpet, praise Him with the harp and lyre, praise Him with tambourine and dancing, praise Him with the strings and flute, praise Him with the clash of cymbals, praise Him with the resounding cymbals. Let everything that has breath praise the Lord. Praise the Lord," (Psalm 150).

New Testament Scripture writers tell of God's worthiness to be praised. The apostle Paul wrote:

"May the God who gives endurance and encouragement give you a spirit of unity among yourselves as you follow Christ Jesus, so that with one heart and mouth you may glorify the God and Father of our Lord Jesus Christ," (Romans 15:5-6).

The author of Hebrews said:

"Through Jesus, therefore, let us continually offer to God a sacrifice of praise-the fruit of lips that confess His name," (Hebrews 13:15).

Throughout the Old and New Testaments, Scriptures offer praises and worship to God. During praise and worship, man uses his voice (mouth), hands and feet as he

Rejoices in Singing

Singing can be expressions of love and thanksgiving to God. It puts man's focus on God and His goodness only. Since Old Testament times, Men have sang songs of praise to acknowledge God for all His goodness. Even when there are struggles in his life, God still deserves the praises. Paul and Silas were in prison and they were praying and singing hymns to God (Acts 16:25). David, the psalmist, wrote:

> "I will praise you, O Lord, with all my heart; before the 'gods' I will sing your praise, and will praise your name for your love and your faithfulness, for you have exalted above all things your name and your word," (Psalm 138:1-2).

> "Praise the Lord. How good it is to sing praises to our God, how pleasant and fitting to praise Him," (Psalm 147:1).

Another psalmist wrote:

> "For you make me glad by your deeds, O Lord; I sing for joy at the works of your hands," (Psalm 92:4).

During his song of praise, the prophet Isaiah said:

> "Sing to the Lord, for He has done glorious things; let this be known to all the world," (Isaiah 12:5).

In the New Testament, authors wrote about singing hymns to worship God. The apostle Paul said:

> "Sing and make music in your heart to the Lord," (Ephesians 5:19b).

"Let the word of Christ dwell in you richly as you teach and admonish one another with all wisdom, and as you sing psalms, hymns and spiritual songs with gratitude in your hearts to God," (Colossians 3:16).

The use of hands and feet are helpful to make a joyful noise to the Lord in worship services. In both the Old and New Testaments, Scriptures tell of men using their hands and feet as they engaged in praise and worship to God. The temple assistants said in their psalm:

"Clap your hands, all you nations; shout to God with cries of joy," (Psalm 47:1).

The psalmist David said:

"I will praise you as long as I live, and in your name I will lift my hands," (Psalm 63:4).

Anonymous Psalmists wrote:

"Come, let us bow down in worship, let us kneel before the Lord our Maker," (Psalm 95:6)

"Let them praise His name with dancing and make music to Him with tambourine and harp," (Psalm 149:3).

The apostle Paul wrote in his first letter to Timothy:

"I want men everywhere to lift up holy hands in prayer, without anger or disputing," (1Timothy 2:8).

Musical instruments have been used to worship and praise God since the Old Testament Days. An anonymous psalmist wrote:

"Praise Him with the sounding of the trumpet. Praise Him with tambourine and dancing, praise Him with the strings and flute, praise Him with the clash of cymbals, praise Him with the resounding cymbals," (Psalm 150:3a, 4-5).

Gives Willingly

Giving is an act of worship when it is done out of love. God gave the world the best gift of all when He gave His Son Jesus Christ to die for the sins of the world. Being a Christian, it is expected of him to give. When he gives with the right motives, he is letting God know that he thanks and appreciate what He has given to him, and now he is able to share with others. Although man is obligated to give, his motives for giving should be pure and honest. He should give according to how God has blessed him. David realized that all that he had and was came from the Lord, and he was able to put things in the proper perspective, when he praised God openly after giving of his personal treasure for the temple of God. He said:

"But who am I, and who are my people, that we should be able to give as generously as this? Everything comes from you, and we have given you only what comes from your hand," (1 Chronicles 29:14).

God told Moses to tell the people:

"No man should come before the Lord empty-handed. Each of you must bring a gift in proportion to the way the Lord your God has blessed you," (Deuteronomy 16:16b-17).

God acknowledges sacrificial and generous giving from the heart. Jesus was in the temple when he saw the rich man and a poor widow putting their gifts in the temple treasury. She put in two small copper coins. Jesus said:

> "This poor widow has put in more than all the others.
> All these people gave their gifts out of their wealth;
> but she out of her poverty put in all she to live on,"
> (Luke 21:1-4).

God is the giver of all good things, and man should not only give of his resources, but he should give of his time and talent. Giving is not about the giver; it is about God. God expects man to be cheerful in his giving whatever he is giving, whether it is the form of monetary or rendering service to others. When man renders service to others, he is also serving God. His deeds should not be to impress anyone, or to make himself look good, but it should be to honor God. In both the Old and New Testaments, Scriptures reveal that God commanded man to give to Him and to others. God told Moses to tell the Israelites:

> "If there is a poor man among your brothers in any of
> the towns of the land that the Lord your God is giving
> you, do not be hardhearted or tightfisted toward your
> poor brother. Rather be openhanded and freely lend
> him whatever he needs," (Deuteronomy 15:7-8).

The psalmist David said:

> "The wicked borrow and do not repay, but the
> righteous give generously," (Psalm 37:21).

Solomon wrote in his words of wisdom:

> "A generous man will himself be blessed, for he shares
> his food with the poor," (Proverbs 22:9).

Jesus taught His disciples that there is a blessing in giving when He said:

"When you give to the needy, do not let your left hand know what your right hand is doing, so that your giving may be in secret. Then your Father, who sees what is done in secret, will reward you openly," (Matthew 6:3-4).

"Give, and it will be given to you. A good measure, pressed down, shaken together and running over, will be poured in your lap. For with the measure you use, it will be measured to you," (Luke 6:38).

"It is more blessed to give than to receive," (Acts 20:35b).

The apostle Paul wrote:

"Whoever sows sparingly will also reap sparingly, and whoever sows generously will also reap generously. Each man should give what he has decided in his heart to give, not reluctantly or under compulsion, for God loves a cheerful giver," (2 Corinthians 9:6-7).

Evangelizes

Evangelizing is telling others about the love of God. The Christian should speak of God's love every opportunity he gets, never making the assumption that someone does not want to know about the love God has for him, or that someone is already a believer. Not only should the believer witness with words, but he must also do it with his living. Since Jesus died on the cross for the sins of the world, every person on this earth deserves to know that Jesus loves him. So when the opportunity presents itself, the believer must not be selective as to whom he is going to witness too. Every person on the face of this earth is God's creation. Jesus gave what is called today, the "Great

Commission" to His disciples, and it is applicable to all believers today. He said to them:

> "Go into all the world and preach the good news to all creation. Whoever believes and is baptized will be saved, but whoever does not believe will be condemned," (Mark 16:15-16).

Christian should look for opportunities to tell others of God's goodness. Although planned sessions for witnessing are great, some opportunities for witnessing are spontaneous. Often times the Holy Spirit will present opportunities for witnessing of God's love. When this happens, the Christian must take advantage of that opportunity. New Testament Scriptures make it clear that God's people must evangelize. Before Jesus' Death, He told His disciples:

> "But you shall receive power when the Holy Spirit has come upon you; and you shall be witnesses to Me in Jerusalem, and in all Judea and Samaria, and to the end of the earth," (Acts 1:8).

The apostle Paul said:

> "Preach the Word; be prepared in season and out of season; correct, rebuke and encourage-with great patience and careful instruction. The time will come when men will not put up with sound doctrine. Instead, to suit their own desire, they will gather around them a great number of teachers to say what their itching ears want to hear. They will turn their ears away from the truth and turn aside to myths. You, keep your head in all situations, endure hardship, do the work of an evangelist," (2 Timothy 4:2-5a).

Partakes of the Lord's Supper

God is being honored whenever the Body of Christ participates in the Lord's Supper. The Lord's Supper is a celebration of Jesus' death on the cross for the sins of the world. It allows God's people to reflect back on what God has done for them; remembering Jesus' death on the cross to save humankind from their sins. This celebration also includes honoring the Father in heaven who instituted the event. The Lord's Supper is very important to Christians, as they believe Jesus commanded them to make this a practice of participating in this great event as often as possible. It was during the Passover Meal that Jesus broke bread and passed the cup to His disciples. The apostle Paul wrote that Jesus said:

> "This cup is the new covenant in my blood; do this, whenever you drink it, in remembrance of me. For whenever you eat this bread and drink this cup, you proclaim the Lord's death until He comes," (1 Corinthians 11:23b-26).

Matthew, the Gospel writer recorded that while Jesus and the disciples were eating the Passover Meal, Jesus took bread, gave thanks, broke it, then gave it to His disciples telling them to eat, "This is my body." Then He took the cup, gave thanks and offered it to them, saying:

> "Drink from it, all of you. This is my blood of the covenant, which is poured out for many for the forgiveness of sins," (Matthew 26:26-28).

Luke recorded that Jesus took the bread, gave thanks, broke it and gave it to them saying:

> "This is my body given for you; do this in remembrance of me," (Luke 22:19).

This practice of partaking in the Lord's Supper has been adopted as one of the Christian churches' ordinances because they believe that Jesus commanded them to do so. A designated amount of time was not set for this to take place, but Paul recorded that Jesus said when He broke the bread and took the cup:

> "Take, eat, this is My body which is broken for you; do this in remembrance of Me. This cup is the new covenant in My blood. This do, as often as you drink it, in remembrance of Me," (1 Corinthians 11:24-25).

Lives a Life of Holiness

God's people are transformed from sinners to saints; therefore, they are new creatures in Christ. Their walk and talk are new, as they represent their obedience to God's Word. The apostle Paul said:

> "Do not conform any longer to the pattern of their world, but be transformed by the renewing of your mind. Then you will be able to test and approve what God's will is, His good, pleasing perfect will," (Romans 12:2).

The new life is a testimony of the choice man has made to make Jesus Christ the Lord of his life. Scriptures in the New Testament tell how God's holy people live so that their living honors and worships Him. The apostle Paul said: "Offer your bodies as living sacrifices, holy and pleasing to God-this is your spiritual act of worship," (Romans 12:1). He also said: "Be made new in the attitude of your minds; and to put on the new self, created to be like God in true righteousness and holiness," (Ephesians 4:23). The apostles Peter and John said:

> "As obedient children, do not conform to the evil desires you had when you lived in ignorance. But just

as He who called you to be holy, so be holy in all you do," (1 Peter 1:15).

"If anyone obeys His Word, God's love is truly made complete in Him. This is how we know we are in Him: Whoever claims to live in Him must walk as Jesus did," (1 John 2:5-6).

Living a holy and righteous life is not always easy because of the many distractions of this world, but it is possible through the work of the Holy Spirit who lives inside the believer.

NEW LIFE IN CHRIST

After being adopted into the family of God, the Christian has a new life in Christ Jesus. He adopts new character traits that represent Christ Jesus. He is not perfect, but is striving for perfection. It is his goal to be more like Jesus every day of his life. The apostle Paul along with other New Testament writers wrote of what the Christian is and what he does in this new life in Christ. They wrote that the believer:

Is Dead to Sin but Alive in Jesus Christ

He counts himself dead to sin but alive to God in Christ Jesus. Therefore, he does not let sin reign in his mortal body to obey its evil desires. He does not offer the parts of his body to sin, as instruments of wickedness, but rather offer himself to God, as those who have been brought from death to life; and offer the parts of his body to Him as instruments of righteousness (Romans 6:11-13).

Lives by the Spirit

He lives by the Spirit, and, therefore, does not gratify the desires of the sinful nature. For the sinful nature desires what is contrary to the Spirit and the Spirit what is contrary to the sinful nature. They are in conflict with each other. He will be led by the Holy Spirit to do what is right in the sight of God (Galatians 5:16-17).

Submits to God

He submits himself to God. He resists the devil so that the devil will flee from him. He comes near to God and He will come near to him. He humbles himself before the Lord, so that he will be lifted up (James 4:7-8, 10).

Rejoices in the Lord

He rejoices in the Lord. He lets his gentleness be evident to all. Because the Lord is near him, he is not to be anxious about anything, but in everything, by prayer and petition, with thanksgiving, presents his request to God. And the peace of God, which transcends all understanding, will guard his heart and his mind in Christ Jesus (Philippians 4:4-7).

Lives a Life of Righteousness

The Christian's mind is set on things above, not on earthly things, for he died to sin, and his life is now hidden with Christ in God. He has put to death whatever belongs to the earthly nature; sexual immorality, impurity, lust, evil desires and greed. He has ridden himself of all such things as these; anger, rage, malice, slander and filthy language from his lips. He does not lie to others, because he has taken his old self off with its practices.

As a Christian, he has clothed himself with compassion, kindness, humility, gentleness and patience. He bears with others and forgives whatever grievances he may have against another. He forgives as the Lord forgave him. And most of all, he shows love to everyone. He lets the peace of Christ rule in his heart, since as a member of one body he was called to peace. He is thankful for all things! He lets the Word of Christ dwell in him richly as he teaches and admonishes others with all wisdom and as he sing psalms, hymns and spiritual songs with gratitude in his hearts to God. And whatever he does, whether in word or deed, he does it all in the name of the Lord Jesus, giving thanks to God the Father through Him (Colossians 3:2, 5-17).

Thinks on the Things of God

With his new mindset, he now fills his mind with the things of Christ by thinking on, "Whatever is true, whatever is noble, whatever is right, whatever is pure, whatever is lovely, whatever is admirable-if anything is excellent or praiseworthy-think about such things," (Philippians 4:8).

Behaves as a Child of God

He puts off falsehood and speaks truthfully to his neighbor. In his anger, he does not sin. He steals no more, but will work, doing something useful with his own hands that he may have something to share with those in need. Unwholesome talk does not come out of his mouth, but only what is helpful for building others up according to their needs. He does not grieve the Holy Spirit of God, with whom he was sealed for the day of redemption. He is rid of all bitterness, rage and anger, brawling and slander, along with every form of malice. He is kind and compassionate.

He is an imitator of God, living a life of love. There will not be even a hint of sexual immorality, or of any kind of impurity, or greed, because these are improper for God's holy people. Obscenity, foolish talk or coarse joking, are out of place, but rather thanksgiving. He is very careful then how he lives-not as unwise but as wise, making the most of every opportunity, because the days are evil. Therefore, he will not be foolish, but understand what the Lord's will is. He will not get drunk on wine, which leads to debauchery. Instead, he will be filled with the Spirit. He sings and makes music in his heart to the Lord; always give thanks to God the Father for everything, in the name of our Lord Jesus Christ. He submits to others out of reverence for Christ (Ephesians 4:25-5:1-4, 15-21).

Acknowledges the Need of Jesus Christ before Men

When he is in trouble, he prays. When he is happy, he sings songs of praise. If he is sick, he calls for the elders of the church to pray over him and anoint him with oil in the name of the Lord, and the prayer offered in faith will make the sick well; the Lord will raise him up. If he has sinned, he will ask to be forgiven (James 5:13-15).

Lives out Love

He knows love must be sincere. He hates what is evil; clings to what is good. He is devoted to others in brotherly love. He honors those above himself. He will never be lacking in zeal, but will keep his spiritual fervor, serving the Lord. He is joyful in hope, patient in affliction and faithful in prayer. He shares with God's people who are in need. He practices hospitality. He blesses those who persecute him; he blesses and does not curse. He rejoices with those who rejoice; mourns with those who mourn. He lives in harmony with others. He is not proud, but is willing to associate with people of low position. He is not conceited. He does not repay anyone evil for evil. He is careful to do what is right in the eyes of everybody. He lives at peace with everyone where it is possible. He is careful not to take revenge, but leaves room for God's wrath. If his enemy is hungry, he feeds him; if he is thirsty, he gives him something to drink. He will not be overcome by evil, but overcomes evil with good (Romans 12:9-21).

He loves every man as a brother. He should not forget to entertain strangers, for by so doing, some people have entertained angels without knowing it. He should remember those in prison as if he were their fellow prisoners, and those who are mistreated as if he himself was suffering (Hebrews 13:1-3).

If someone is caught in a sin, he being spiritual should restore him gently. But he must watch himself, or he may be tempted. He carries the burdens of others, and in this way he will fulfill the law of Christ (Galatians 6:1-2).

Is Agreeable

The Christian tries to get along with everyone, saved or not. He puts forth the effort to do everything without complaining or arguing. He knows how to disagree without being disagreeable (Philippians 2:14).

Honors Family Relationships

Wives are to submit to their husbands, as is fitting in the Lord. Husbands will love their wives and will not be harsh with them. Children will obey their parents in everything, for this pleases the Lord. Fathers will not embitter their children, or they will become discouraged (Colossians 3:18-21).

Marriage should be honored by all, and the marriage bed is kept pure, for God will judge the adulterer and all the sexually immoral (Hebrews 13:5).

Respects Others

He respects those who work hard among him, who is over him in the Lord and who admonishes him. He holds them in the highest regard in love because of their work. He lives in peace with others. He should warn his brothers who are idle, encourage the timid, help the weak, be patient with everyone. He makes sure that he does not pay back wrong for wrong, but always try to be kind to everyone. He holds onto the good and avoids every kind of evil (1 Thessalonians 5:12-22).

CHAPTER SEVEN

Eternal Life

"Eternal life is a person's new and redeemed existence in Jesus Christ, which is granted by God as a gift to all believers," (Nelson's Illustrated Bible Dictionary). Since eternal life is a gift of God, it cannot be earned, bought or sold. It is given to those who accept Jesus Christ as Lord and Savior, and are obedient to God's Word. All believers; those that are dead, and those that are alive when Jesus returns will live with Him forever. Eternal life is not an extension of life on earth as we know it to be now. It is based on the life that the believer will enjoy forever in the presence of the Almighty God. Jesus promised eternal life to all who believed in Him when He said:

> "Those who do not believe will go away to eternal punishment. Those who believe will have eternal life (Matthew 26:46).

> "Whoever hears my words and believes Him who sent me has eternal life and will not be condemned; he has crossed over from death to life," (John 5:24).

> "For God so loved the world that He gave His one and only Son, that whoever believes in Him shall not perish but have eternal life," (John 3:16).

The children of God do not understand in its entirety of their future, but they do know that being in the family of God, they will one day spend eternal life with the Lord. The apostle John wrote that Jesus said:

> "Do not let your heart be troubled. Trust in God; trust also in me. In my Father's house are many rooms; if it were not so, I would have told you. I am going there to prepare a place for you. And if I go and prepare a place for you, I will come back and take you to be with me that you may also be where I am," (John 14:1).

> "We are children of God, and what we will be has not yet been made known. But we know that when He appears, we shall be like Him, for we shall see Him as He is," (1 John 3:2).

Just as Jesus had to die and be resurrected before He could send back the Holy Spirit as a Comforter, He also had to die and be resurrected in order for humankind to spend eternal life with Him. His death on the cross, His resurrection, His ascension back to heaven, and the sending of the Comforter, all prepared the way for eternal life for the believer.

Eternal life was not a new concept to the New Testament. When God's Spirit leaves man, he dies. His body goes back to the dust from which it came, but the spirit and soul will live forever because it will return back to God who gave it. In the beginning, God told Adam that he would return to the ground because he was taken from it, and that he was dust and to dust he would return (Genesis 3:19b). Solomon, the son of King David, said:

> "The dust returns to the ground it came from, and the spirit returns to God who gave it,"
>
> (Ecclesiastes 12:7).

Scriptures in both the Old and New Testaments reveal that Bible characters spoke of their being with the Lord when life was over on this earth.

Job said in a conversation with his three friends:

> "I know that my Redeemer lives, and that in the end He will stand upon the earth. And after my skin has been destroyed, yet in my flesh I will see God; I myself will see him with my own eyes-I and not another. How my heart yearns within," (Job 19:25-26).

The psalmist David wrote:

> "My heart is glad and my tongue rejoices; my body also will rest secure, because you will not abandon me to the grave, nor will you let your holy one see decay. You have made known to me the path of life; you will fill me with joy in your presence, with eternal pleasures at your right hand," (Psalm 16:9-11).

God said to Daniel in one of his last visions:

> "Multitudes who sleep in the dust of the earth will awake, some to everlasting life, others to shame and everlasting contempt," (Daniel 12:2).

The apostle Paul assured believers of eternal life when he said:

> "But now that you have been set free from sin and have become slaves to God, the benefit you reap leads to holiness, and the result is eternal life. For the wages of sin is death, but the gift of God is eternal life in Christ Jesus our Lord," (Romans 6:22-23).

According to Scriptures, all people of the world are going to spend an eternity in either heaven or in the lake of fire (Revelation 20:15). Jesus will reign until all enemies are destroyed. Then the world as man knows it finally comes to an end. Jesus will then hand over the kingdom of God to God the Father, after He has destroyed all dominion, authority and power, and lastly death (1 Corinthians 15:24-26).

While on the Isle of Patmos, God revealed to John in a vision; The Second Coming of Jesus Christ; Satan's Doom; the Judgment; and the New Heaven and Earth (Revelation 19:11-21:6).

THE SECOND COMING OF JESUS CHRIST

The Bible proclaims that Jesus is coming back again, as that is the only way Christians will be able to spend eternal life with God. His appearing this time will be called, "His Second Coming," and at that time He will be coming back for the saints of God. Jesus said, "You must also be ready, because the Son of Man will come at an hour when you do not expect Him," (Luke 12:40). Man does not know the day or hour of His return, but the Bible says He is coming back again. Jesus' disciples came to Him privately wanting to know about the time of His second coming. They asked, "What will be the sign of your coming and of the end of the age?" Jesus gave them signs when He said:

> "Watch out that no one deceives you. For many will come in my name, claiming, 'I am the Christ,' and will deceive many. You will hear of rumors of wars. Nation will rise against nation, and kingdom against kingdom. There will be famines and earthquakes in various places. False Christ and false prophets will appear and perform great signs and miracles to deceive even the elect, if that were possible," (Matthew 24:3-7, 24).

Jesus assured man of His Second Coming when He said:

> "They will see the Son of Man coming on the clouds
> of the sky, with power and great glory, and He will
> send His angels with a loud trumpet call, and they will
> gather His elect from the four winds, from one end
> of the heavens to the other," (Matthew 24:30b-31).

> "In the future, you will see the Son of Man sitting at
> the right hand of the Mighty One and coming on the
> clouds of heaven," (Matthew 26:64).

Jesus told His disciples to remain watchful because, "No one knows about that day or hour, not even the angels in heaven, nor the Son, but only the Father," (Matthew 24:36). Although no one knows when Jesus will return, Old Testament writers wrote of Jesus' Second Coming before His birth. The prophet Isaiah said:

> "See, the day of the Lord is coming, a cruel day, with
> wrath and fierce anger to make the land desolate and
> destroy the sinners within it. The stars of heaven and
> their constellations will not show their light. The
> rising sun will be darkened and the moon will not
> give its light," (Isaiah 13:9-10).

The prophet Daniel had a vision that revealed that the Messiah will come and be the ruler of the spiritual kingdom. He said:

> "In my vision at night I looked, and there before me
> was one like a Son of Man, coming with the clouds of
> heaven. He approached the Ancient of Days and was
> led into His presence. He was given authority, glory
> and sovereign power; all peoples, nations and men of
> every language worshiped Him. His dominion is an
> everlasting dominion that will not pass away, and His

kingdom is one that will never be destroyed," (Daniel 7:13-14).

New Testament Scriptures also support the Second Coming of Jesus Christ. Luke recorded that as Jesus was taken up before the very eyes of His disciples, He was hidden by the clouds, as they stood staring into the sky. Two men dressed in white stood beside them and said:

> "Men of Galilee, why do you stand here looking into the sky? This same Jesus, who has been taken from you into heaven, will come back in the same way you have seen him go into heaven," (Acts 1:8-11).

The apostle Paul wrote:

> "The Lord Himself will come down from heaven, with a loud command, with the voice of the archangel and with the trumpet call of God," (1 Thessalonians 4:15a).

Jesus has to reign until all evil is defeated on this earth. In John's vision, in the last scene on earth, he sees heaven open up and Jesus appears with the angels following Him. The antichrist and his forces gathered to make war against Jesus and His angels. They are captured and thrown alive into the fiery lake of burning sulfur (Revelation 19:11-20). After Jesus has destroyed all the enemies, including death, He will hand over the kingdom to God the Father (1 Corinthians 15:24-26).

THE DESTRUCTION OF SATAN

Although Satan is "the prince of this world," he is destined to fail because he does not have the power to stand up against God's power. He and his power over death in this world will come to an end. His reign will be over at Jesus' second return. John saw in his vision where an angel came down out of heaven with the key to the Abyss (bottomless pit), and holding a great chain. Satan is seized and is bound for one thousand years. The angel threw him into the Abyss, and locked and sealed it to keep him from deceiving the world anymore until the thousand years have ended. After that, he must be set free for a short time (Revelation 20:1-3).

When the thousand years are over, Satan will be released from the bottomless pit, and will go out and deceive people again into sinning against God. The evil forces will band together to go in battle against God, but fire from heaven will come down and kill them. Satan will then be thrown into the lake of burning sulfur where the antichrist and his evil forces are. There, they will be tormented day and night forever and ever (Revelation 20:7-10). Other New Testament Scriptures verify the destruction of Satan. Jesus said:

> "Now is the time for judgment on this world; now the prince of this world will be driven out," (John 12:31).

The apostle Paul said:

> "The God of peace will soon crush Satan under your feet," (Romans 16:20a).

When Satan and all his evil forces no longer exist, there will be nothing to separate God and His people. Death is not powerful enough to keep God and His people apart. The apostle Paul said:

> "For I am convinced that neither death nor life, neither angels nor demons, neither the present nor the future, nor any powers, neither height nor depth, nor anything else in all creation, will be able to separate us from the love of God that is in Christ Jesus our Lord," (Romans 8:38-39).

THE RESURRECTION OF THE SAINTS OF GOD

Our Lord and Savior Jesus Christ was resurrected from the dead by God, so will all believers be resurrected from their physical death. When Jesus returns, some will be dead, while others will be alive. According to Paul, the dead in Christ will rise first. He said, "We believe that Jesus died and rose again and so we believe that God will bring with Jesus those who have fallen asleep in Him," (1 Thessalonians 4:14). Paul says that the Saints of God will be given new bodies when Christ returns, as they will be raised imperishable for the perishable must clothe itself with the imperishable, and the mortal with immortality (1 Corinthians 15:52b-53). The new bodies will be glorified bodies, that is, they will be perfect. Scripture writers wrote of the dead being resurrected in both the Old and New Testaments. The psalmist David wrote of his joy in knowing that he would be resurrected from the dead when he said:

> "Therefore my heart is glad and my tongue rejoices; my body also will rest secure, because you will not abandon me to the grave, nor will you let your Holy One see decay," (Psalm 16:9-11).

In his prophetic book of the Bible, Daniel said:

> "Multitudes who sleep in the dust of the earth will awake: Some to everlasting life, others to shame and everlasting contempt," (Daniel 12:2).

Jesus said:

> "A time is coming when all who are in their graves will hear His voice and come out. Those who have done good will rise to live, and those who have done evil will rise to be condemned," (John 5:28-29).

The apostle Paul wrote:

> "For the Lord Himself will come down from heaven, with a loud command, with the voice of the archangel and with the trumpet call of God, and the dead in Christ will rise first," (1Thessalonians 4:16).

> "The trumpet will sound, the dead will be raised imperishable," (1 Corinthians 15:52b).

The Rapture

According to the Bible, all the saints of God will not die before Jesus' Second Coming. Although the dead in Christ will be resurrected first, the Bible declares that those that are alive when Jesus comes back will be with Him. The apostle Paul said that when the Lord comes from heaven, the dead in Christ shall rise first. Then he said, "After that, we who are still alive and are left will be caught up together with them in the clouds to meet the Lord in the air," (1 Thessalonians 4:16-17).

The term, "The Rapture" is not found in the Bible, but theologians and Bible scholars refer to this "Being caught up together with them in the clouds to meet the Lord in the air" as "The Rapture." In regards to what theologians refer to as "The Rapture," Paul said:

> "We will not all sleep, but we will all be changed-in a flash, in the twinkling of an eye, at the last trumpet," (1 Corinthians 15:51b-52a).

> "According to the Lord's own words, we tell you that we who are still alive, who are left till the coming of the Lord, will certainly not precede those who have fallen asleep," (1 Thessalonians 4:15).

The Resurrected Bodies of the Saints

The resurrected bodies of the saints will be transformed. The apostle Paul said flesh and blood cannot enter into the kingdom of God because it is not suitable for eternity. God will give every believer in Him a new body upon his resurrection. Each body will be raised imperishable, in glory, in power and spiritual (1 Corinthians 15:42-44).

Glorified Bodies

This new body is called a glorified body because it is going to be just like Jesus' body which is completely perfect. It will be spiritual and have no limitations. It will be made to last forever. It will never get sick or weak, and will never die. The apostle Paul wrote that the new body will be raised imperishable, never to be perishable again; raised in glory, never to be in dishonor again; raised in power, never to be weak again; and is spiritual, never to be natural again (1 Corinthians 15:42-44). He also wrote:

> "It is by the power of the Lord Jesus Christ that enables Him to bring everything under His control, will transform our lowly bodies so that they will be like His glorious body," (Philippians 3:21).

THE FINAL JUDGMENT

The final judgment will include all people and nations from the beginning of the world to the end of time. Jesus will return to earth and will judge all people, according to God's standards. According to the Gospel writer Luke, Jesus will be the righteous judge during the final judgment. God appointed Him to judge, and has set a day aside when He will judge the world with justice (Acts 17:31b). The apostle Paul said that God commanded them to preach to the people and to testify that Jesus is the One whom God appointed as judge of the living and the dead (Acts 10:42). He also said in regards to Jesus' judgment:

> "He will punish those who do not know God and do not obey the gospel of our Lord Jesus. They will be punished with everlasting destruction and shut out from the presence of the Lord and from the majesty of His power," (2 Thessalonians 1:8-9).

Judgment Day

On the Day of Judgment, the dead and those that are alive will come together to be judged according to what they have done. The apostle John wrote:

> "The sea gave up the dead that were in it, and death and Hades gave up the dead that were in them, and each person was judged according to what he had done," (Revelation 20:13).

The separation of the good and the bad takes place, and will consequently end the old way of living. The apostle Peter refers to the Day of Judgment as "The Day of the Lord" (2 Peter3:10). Both Old and New Testament characters spoke about a Judgment Day for all people. In his message to the people, the prophet Obadiah said:

> "The day of the Lord is near for all nations. As you have done, it will be done to you; your deeds will return upon your own head," (Obadiah 15).

The Bible says that Jesus said:

> "For the Son of Man is going to come in His Father's glory with His angels, and then He will reward each person according to what he has done," (Matthew 16:27-28).

The apostle Paul wrote:

> "We will all stand before God's judgment seat. It is written: 'As surely as I live, says the Lord, every knee will bow before Me; every tongue will confess to God.' So then, each of us will give an account of himself to God," (Romans 14:10b-12).

> "For we must all appear before the judgment seat of Christ, that each one may receive what is due him for the things done while in the body, whether good or bad," (2 Corinthians 5:10).

The author of Hebrews said:

> "Just as man is destined to die once, and after that, he is to face judgment," (Hebrews 9:27).

The Book of Life

The Book of Life is a heavenly book that will be opened at the judgment. It will contain the names of everyone who have accepted Jesus Christ as their Lord and Savior. It is a record of who belongs to Him. The names of those that appear in the Lamb's book of life will enter into the New Heavens and earth to live eternally with God, the Father. The names of those that are not recorded in the Lamb's book of life will be recorded in another book and they will be condemned because they did not believe in the Lord Jesus Christ. John wrote:

> "I saw a great white throne and Him who was seated on it. And I saw the dead great and small, standing before the throne, and books were opened. Another book was opened, which is the book of life. The dead were judged according to what they had done as recorded in the books. If anyone's name was not

found written in the book of life, he was thrown into
the lake of fire," (Revelation 20:11-12, 15).

At the end of John's visions, an angel gave the message of Jesus when
He said:

> "Behold, I am coming soon! My reward is with me,
> and I will give to everyone according to what He has
> done," (Revelation 22:12).

THE NEW HEAVEN AND EARTH

God began the Book of Genesis, the first book of the Bible with
the creation of the heavens and the earth. The Book of Revelation,
the last book of the Bible, tells us that God the Creator of the heavens
and earth will be destroying it. He will then create a new heaven and
a new earth for His people to live with Him forever, one that is free of
sin and evilness. The new heaven and earth will appear after the old
heaven disappears and the old earth is burned up (2 Peter 3:10). God
is coming down from heaven to dwell with His people. The apostle
John said:

> "I saw a new heaven and a new earth, for the first
> heaven and the first earth had passed away. I saw
> the Holy City, the New Jerusalem, coming down out
> of heaven from God, prepared as a bride beautifully
> dressed for her husband. And I heard a loud voice
> from the throne saying, 'Now the dwelling of God is
> with men, and He will live with them. They will be
> His people, and God Himself will be with them and
> be their God,'" (Revelation 21:1-3).

God's people do not know everything there is to know about the
new heaven and earth, but we do know that according to the Bible,
there will be one, and that God's people will be with Him. It will

be the home of those whose names are listed in the Book of Life. The righteous men and women of God will receive their heavenly citizenship. It is going to be large enough to hold all God's people and it will last for eternity. Writers in both the Old and New Testaments addressed the fact that there will be a new heaven and earth. God told the prophet Isaiah:

> "Behold, I will create new heavens and a new earth. The former things will not be remembered, nor will they come to mind. But be glad and rejoice forever in what I will create, for I will create Jerusalem and take delight in my people; the sound of weeping and of crying will be heard in it no more," (Isaiah 65:17-19).

The apostle Peter wrote in his second letter:

> "But in keeping with His promise we are looking forward to a new heaven and a new earth, the home of righteousness," (2 Peter 3:13).

The apostle John said in his vision:

> "I heard a loud voice from the throne saying, 'Now the dwelling of God is with men, and he will live with them. They will be His people, and God Himself will be with them and be their God," (Rev. 21:3).

LIFE IN THE NEW HEAVEN AND EARTH

Life in the new heaven and earth is not going to be an extension of the old life. Every thing is going to be new as the old heaven and earth will be destroyed. God told John in his vision that He was going to make everything new (Revelation 21:5). Life in the new heaven and earth is going to be perfect as we will be like Jesus Christ. This is what Scriptures say about life in the new heaven and earth:

Man Will Live in the Presence of God

John, the revelator, wrote that he heard a loud voice from the throne saying:

> "Now the dwelling of God is with men, and He will live with them. They will be His people, and God Himself will be with them and be their God," (Revelation 21:3).

Man Will Be like Jesus

The apostle Paul recorded:

> "And just as we have borne the likeness of the earthly man, so shall we bear the likeness of the man from heaven," (1 Corinthians 15:49).

The apostle John wrote in his first letter:

> "Dear friend, now we are children of God, and what we will be has not yet been made known. But we know that when He appears, we shall be like Him, for we shall see Him as He is," (1John 3:2).

Death Will Be Defeated

Jesus said:

> "They can no longer die; for they are like the angels. They are God's children, since they are children of the resurrection," (Luke 20:36).

The apostle Paul said:

> "The last enemy to be destroyed is death,"
> (1 Corinthians 15:26).

No More Sorrow or Sickness

The new glorified body will never get weak, will never get sick and will never die. In John's vision, he heard a loud voice from the throne saying:

> "He will wipe every tear from their eyes. There will
> be no more death or mourning or crying or pain, for
> the old order of things has passed away," (Revelation
> 21:4).

No Need for Temples or Churches

John did not see a temple in the New Jerusalem because there will be no need for one. God's presence will be everywhere, and His people will be in constant praise of Him. He said:

> "I did not see a temple in the city, because the
> Lord God Almighty and the Lamb are its temple,"
> (Revelation 21:22).

No More Darkness

In John's vision, the angel said:

> "The city does not need the sun or the moon to shine
> on it, for the glory of God gives it light, and the Lamb
> is its lamp," (Revelation 21:23).

"There will be no more night. They will not need the light of a lamp or the light of the sun, for the Lord God will give them light," (Revelation 22:5).

No Impurities

In John' vision, the angel said:

"Nothing impure will ever enter into it, nor will anyone who does what is shameful or deceitful, but only those whose names are written in the Lamb's Book of Life," (Revelation 21:27).

No Marriages

Luke recorded that Jesus said:

"The people of this age marry and are given in marriage. But those who are considered worth of taking part in that age and in the resurrection from the dead will neither marry nor be given in marriage, and they can no longer die; for they are like the angels. They are God's children, since they are children of the resurrection," (Luke 20:34-36).

The City Will Be Made of Precious Stones

According to John the Revelator, the New Jerusalem will have walls made of jasper, and the city of pure gold, as pure as glass. The foundation of the city wall will be decorated with every kind of precious stone. Each gate to the city will be made of a single pearl, and the streets of pure gold, like transparent glass. (Revelation 21:18-21).

There Will Be a River of the Water of Life

John also said there will be a river of the water of life, and it is going to be crystal clear, and will be flowing from the throne of God and of the Lamb. It is going to be located in the middle of the great street of the city. The saints will not have to be concerned about their food supply, nor health issues. On each side of the river will be a tree of life bearing twelve crops of fruit, yielding its fruit every month. And the leaves of the tree are for the healing of the nation (Revelation 22:1-2).

There Will Be Eternal Peace

Nothing will be cursed, doomed or destroyed. John, the revelator said: "No longer will there be any curse. The throne of God and of the Lamb will be in the city, and His servants will serve Him," (Revelation 22:3).

Yes, humankind is born into this world with a sinful nature. But by the grace of God, we are able to depart from this world as saved, filled with the Holy Spirit, sanctified, and assured of a heavenly home where we will reside in the presence of the Lord forever.

God's grace gave man salvation by allowing him an opportunity to accept Jesus Christ as his Savior; being justified for his sins, he is then reconciled back with God. Sanctification takes place when the believer is diligently obedient to God's will and His way. Glorification is the final state of the believer after death when he or she becomes like Christ. The stage is finally set for God's people to live with Him forever and ever.

REFERENCES

Life Application Bible-The New International Version; Tyndale House Publishers, Inc., and Zondervan Publishing House, 1991

The Holy Bible, New King James Version; Thomas Nelson, Inc., 1992

Nelson's Illustrated Bible Dictionary; Thomas Nelson Publishers, 1986

Scriptures at Your Fingertips; Howard Books, a Division of Simon and Schuster, Inc., 2006

CPSIA information can be obtained
at www.ICGtesting.com
Printed in the USA
BVHW041103120521
607049BV00004B/385